FRIENDS OF ACPL

REA

241
Fos
LIFE AFTER DIVORCE

3 1833 01901 8354

241.63 F81L
FOSTER, GAYLE C.
LIFE AFTER DIVORCE

OCT 3 '90

ALLEN COUNTY PUBLIC LIBRARY
FORT WAYNE, INDIANA 46802

You may return this book to any agency, branch,
or bookmobile of the Allen County Public Library.

Edited by Marvin Moore
Designed by Tim Larson
Cover Photo by Duane Tank
Type set in 10/12 Century Schoolbook

Copyright © 1987 by
Pacific Press Publishing Association
Printed in United States of America
All Rights Reserved

The author assumes full responsibility for the accuracy of all facts and quotations cited in this book.

Library of Congress Catalog Card Number: 87-62718

ISBN 0-8163-0766-0

87 88 89 90 91 • 5 4 3 2 1

Contents

Dedication and Acknowledgments ... 4
Introduction ... 5
Chapter 1: Suddenly Single ... 7
Chapter 2: The Demands of Living Alone ... 16
Chapter 3: The Sting of Loneliness ... 26
Chapter 4: Are We Still a Family? ... 36
Chapter 5: God's Constant Provisions ... 46
Chapter 6: The Road to the Working World ... 55
Chapter 7: Feeling Good About Yourself ... 64
Chapter 8: Sexuality and New Relationships ... 72
Chapter 9: To Remain Single or to Remarry? ... 80
Epilogue ... 88
Appendix ... 89

Dedication and Acknowledgments

**This book is dedicated
to the Glory and Honor of the Lord**

I also wish to give special recognition:

To my beloved husband, Dick, without whose encouragement this book could not have been written, and who has brought happiness, more than I dreamed possible, into my life.

To Sue Keister, who spent many hours editing my manuscript, and to Mary Brite, who helped with the rewrite.

To my children, Tiffany, David, and Richard, who were patient with me when I was at the typewriter.
To my foster daughters, Cindy and Cathy.

To Chuck and Linda Coker, who shared their knowledge and insights and offered much encouragement, and to Dick and Carol Costen.

And especially to my parents, William and Rosa Carraway, who stood by me "through it all."

Author's note: All of the events described in this book are true. However, the names of some of the principle characters have been changed to protect the children.

Introduction

As God accompanied me through my divorce, He also gently led me in the writing of *Life After Divorce*. Some of the memories were painful as I relived the past, but writing them down had therapeutic value. Several times I've put this material aside and decided not to continue. Each time God brought someone or something into my life to urge me to go on.

Looking back over the years of being alone, I realize that no one could have convinced me earlier that I would ever feel like a whole person again. How often I asked myself back then, "Will things ever be better? Will I ever be happy again?"

It's great to be alive. I never honestly believed I'd feel that way again. But I do! I hope my experiences will help others feel that way again too.

Chapter 1

Suddenly Single

"Once upon a time . . . the prince and the princess were married, . . . and they lived *happily* ever after!" That's what I'd heard, been taught, believed in, and looked forward to all my life. It was my eternal dream. Perhaps it's extremely naive to believe that fairy tale, but I did.

All I ever wanted was to be a good wife and mother. Divorce never entered my plans. In fact, I vowed "it" would *never* happen to me. I would have the perfect marriage—forever and always!

So what happened?

We started out with such good intentions. But somewhere along the way the dream that started our nine-year marriage turned into a nightmare. Our well-situated rented home and the soil it stood on became a battleground. Our hearts grew severely hardened and totally void of kindness.

Outwardly, people thought we were such a happily married couple. After the fabric of the marriage unraveled, I was told, "We're so shocked to hear about you two. We thought you were the ideal couple." That's the way it appeared.

I committed my life to Christ ten months before my marriage ended. I prayed diligently for God to heal our broken relationship. But the harder I tried to make our marriage work, the worse it became. Years later I finally understood that I hadn't turned our marriage over to God. I told Him about our problems, then proceeded to solve them myself. Not God's way, but my way.

I disliked divorce and everything it stood for. I'd seen divorce literally destroy the lives of beautiful individuals. Some lost every shred of hope and self-confidence. They didn't know whom to turn to or where to turn. Bitterness, confusion, despair, emptiness, and guilt prevailed. Obviously, I didn't want to follow in their footsteps. It happened anyway.

I knew that divorce, like any other traumatic change, would open up a whole new set of problems. At that time, I didn't know what kind of problems there'd be or if I'd be able to handle them. I suspected that the adjustments might be severe, but hoped they'd produce less strain than clinging to an unhappy marriage.

Secretly, I blamed my husband for all our problems. Why his endless flirtations? Why his inability to stick with a job for more than eighteen months? Why the need to move from apartment to apartment? What caused his apparent lack of responsibility and our ever-present financial pressures?

We discussed our difficulties with a pastor and a counselor. I learned, through many in-depth sessions, that our problems started in the early stages of our marriage. And much to my surprise, I discovered that my mistakes equaled my husband's. Indeed, we were *both* responsible for the breakdown of our relationship.

When my husband and I separated, my life changed drastically overnight. Everything was different. Trying to make the transition from "married" to "single again" overwhelmed me. All too soon I discovered how unprepared I was for the reality of the separation.

My emotions careened between depression and genuine peace. Peace surfaced because the constant battling and arguing between my husband and me was over. (Well, not completely, but I didn't have to cope with it twenty-four hours a day!) Guilt cast me into an enormous depression during the three years of separation which preceded our divorce. I carried tons of guilt over the failed marriage, over conflicting religious beliefs, and, of course, over the care of my precious children. Was I doing the right thing for them? Would keeping our marriage together strictly for their sake have been better for their growth and development?

We had a four-year-old daughter and a three-month-old son of our own, plus two foster daughters, ages twelve and fourteen, who lived in our home for four years. When we separated, the foster children were placed in another home while I kept our own two. I suffered a great deal of guilt over these two darling foster girls. Not only had they witnessed the demise of their parents' marriage; they'd watched ours die as well.

Before the separation, four children under the same roof caused noise and bustling activity. Now the house seemed quiet in comparison. In fact, the silence was suffocating.

Divorce is a stern instructor. As the new "head of the household," I was forced to take charge of every aspect of our existence. In marriage, my husband had made every important decision. In a way, I was comfortable with that arrangement. How I'd hated to make decisions!

One regrettable but major earlier decision had been putting off my own advanced education in order to help my husband obtain his college degree. Thus when we separated my own marketable skills were grossly outdated. I didn't know how to manage the family finances, balance a checkbook, handle medical or legal obligations, or make long-range plans for employment and financial security.

After the separation I continued making as few decisions as possible, especially those that produced long-range effects on my family. My ability to plan ahead was limited by a lack of both education and finances. I felt devastated trying to figure out what to do in every situation. I was aware, though, that children need the security of warm, familiar surroundings, a scheduled routine, and lots of tender, loving care, so I slowly changed our lifestyle.

My husband supported us completely for the first few months. My father also helped financially and urged me to apply for Aid to Families with Dependent Children, an idea which at first humiliated me. I halfheartedly checked the want ads in the newspaper. Most called for qualifications I didn't have. It was heartbreaking to consider leaving my children every day. I prayed and repeated Romans 8:28 over and over in my mind: "We know that God causes all things to work together for good to those who love God."*—*"All things,"* I reminded myself. I placed my problem in God's hands and struggled to rely on Him, to believe that the best would come out of this "soul-wrenching" experience.

I soon decided to let AFDC be a temporary financial solution, allowing me time to be with my children during their formative years and to develop skills for my future employment. After all, I consoled myself, I'd worked and paid taxes to help others gain these advantages. Now I needed help for a while.

We qualified easily for AFDC and received $221 per month, plus food stamps and Medicaid. My rent was $150 a month. After paying tithe, there was $57 left for the telephone, electricity, and miscellaneous needs. It wasn't easy, but I was at home caring for my children, and that mattered above all else—even pride. As I look back on those early months, I realize that my emotions were in such bad shape I couldn't have functioned in a job anyway.

New sources of frustration came from unexpected areas. A real sense of defeat came from not being able to physically open peanut butter or pickle jars—such a little thing, yet so hard to achieve. Feelings of aloneness and helplessness intensified at these times. It's amazing how something like that can completely throw a person off balance!

I'd always taken for granted that there would be someone around to help. And there had been. As a young girl I lived in the shadow of my parents' love, guidance, and protection. Nurtured, almost from the cradle, to be a wife and mother, I believed that my husband would *always* be my provider and protector.

Unfortunately, the concept of *self-sufficiency* was as absent from my thoughts as were my dreams. Other concepts were equally missing from my thoughts. I certainly neglected to notice how society viewed divorced persons, but that wouldn't have mattered, as I never expected to be one!

---

*Scripture references in this book are from the New American Standard Bible.

Divorced people face intense social stigmas. They are labeled as swingers and free spirits who lack responsibility, caring, morals, and stability. Among the preconceived ideas is one that is particularly negative: that the divorced person "made the choice."

A preacher's wife shared with me that her husband fell in love with a pregnant, unmarried counselee. Though that may not have caused a divorce, the counselee's warning that she'd commit suicide if he didn't take care of her may have had a big impact. I don't know the other side of this story, but I do know that the minister's wife didn't want a divorce, yet people still thought she'd "made" a choice.

Another preconceived notion—one that I shared—was that men had an easier time adjusting to divorce than women. Frankly, I believed they *never* suffered from the emotional, spiritual, and financial struggles the way women did.

My husband, for example, moved back to his parents' home, worked at the same job, and didn't have to cook his own meals or eat alone or even take care of his own clothes. The income that once provided for a family of six was now spent on one person's needs. He seemed to pick up the pieces of his life almost overnight and started to date again. Nothing seemed to bother him. In fact, he appeared to be having a lot of fun. I'm afraid I didn't have much patience with the plight of the divorced male.

But contrasting with my husband's actions, which seemed to confirm my opinions, was Todd's story, which enlightened me to the truth. Todd's account follows:

> I am a thirty-six-year-old male, in the service of my country, who has recently gone through a divorce after fourteen years of marriage and the birth of three children. My friends were supportive of my actions, saying they felt a divorce was better for the children than seeing us fight all the time.
>
> The week before my divorce was final I was transferred to another duty station. I felt sorry for my children and sorry that I had to leave them, but was very glad to get

away from their mother. My children began adapting to life without me.

To keep from declaring bankruptcy after the divorce, I borrowed from various sources to pay off a lot of small loans and charge accounts. My ex was left with only her lawyer's bill, which she covered with the money in a joint savings account we'd set aside for that purpose. She was awarded $100 a month per child. She had the house ($8,000 equity) and a new station wagon. I paid $160 a month on her car loan. Her house note was $250 a month, which child support more than paid.

It will take a little over two years of scrimping, saving, and doing without to pay off these debts.

As far as making adjustments, I've had to resign myself to the fact that my ex will not encourage my children to call or write. At times, this is hard to accept. I send them birthday gifts and do not receive a thank-you note.

Although my life after divorce has been filled with mixed emotions, I feel that a great burden has been lifted from my shoulders. But not the burden of being a father. I still care about my children and want to see them grow up happy.

Todd's story helped me to understand that men react much as women and that there are two sides to every marital separation. He suffered from emotional and financial difficulties just as I did, struggling to adjust to single life, and his problems were compounded by the strangeness of a new duty station.

In most cases, men are the ones who leave familiar surroundings and have to struggle to form new friendships. Women more often have difficulty dealing with money and generating financial independence. We'll discuss that more in the next chapter.

Before we go on to that, though, let's consider guilt and forgiveness. As a Christian who desired to stay within God's will and grace, I felt particularly vulnerable to guilt. Like most divorced people, I allowed it to engulf my life. I was drowning in a sea of guilt, struggling to accept God's unconditional forgiveness. I felt alienated from God, yet at the same time I was desperately grasping for Him as my only life preserver.

Every Christian knows that God hates divorce (see Malachi 2:16), but several of my Christian friends tried to make me believe that divorce was more sinful than any other iniquity. While I do not condone divorce, I believe it should be treated like any other *forgivable* sin. James 2:10 says, "Whoever keeps the whole law and yet stumbles in one point, he has become guilty of all." That includes obesity, greed, and pride, not just divorce.

Yes, God hates divorce, but not divorced *people*. He loves all people. He works in broken relationships to heal and forgive. He meets us where we are. No one is beyond God's reach. He places a high value on every human life, even one we might consider worthless. He looks beyond the wreckage produced by sin and sees enormous potential.

> How can we make constructive use of guilt? First, recognize that guilt is a legitimate emotion. . . . It is an early warning signal to save us from sin and self-defeat. . . . Second, examine guilt's roots. . . . Take a long look at the attitudes and actions causing the guilt. . . . Face the cause honestly. This confronting who we are and what we've done is a necessary part of God's process of healing. . . . Third, accept forgiveness. God is offering it. The price? Confession, repentance, and possibly restitution. . . . Finally, forgive yourself. That's not as hard as it might seem. . . . Focus on these words: "Because God has forgiven me, I forgive me too." Then do it.[1]

Suggestions for Helping Yourself to Good Healing

Dwell on the present, not the past. Accept reality—the marriage is over! Let go of your former mate. It's the most healthy and loving thing you can do for yourself, for any children involved, and for your ex-spouse.

---

1. An Underground Manual for Spiritual Survival. Copyrighted Larry E. Neagle. Used by Permission.

Count today's blessings. (Oh, no, you think, not again. But it *is* beneficial!) Thank God frequently for the positive aspects of your past marital experience. Children may be the *best* dividends of a marriage, but good comes out of any loving relationship, no matter how short, even if it was only a temporary ego boost.

When you reach a point where a choice is possible, choose to stop grieving. It's normal to mourn the death of a relationship and to suffer temporarily from a setback, but don't allow this period of mourning to last indefinitely. Grief that persists beyond two years may indicate that professional advice is needed.

Let your mind *dwell* on these things: "Whatever is true, whatever is honorable, whatever is right, whatever is pure, whatever is lovely, whatever is of good repute." Philippians 4:8.

Do something you've always wanted to do. Make a number of short-range plans. Set several realistic goals to focus on and to work toward; then reward yourself when you attain one of them.

Keep busy. Write letters. Get out of the house or apartment, get a job, or do volunteer work. Read books by others who have survived divorce. Attend a workshop, get a college degree, take lessons in photography or music. What's the secret desire of your heart? Work to achieve it.

Above all else, *be proud of your accomplishments,* regardless of how simple. Some mornings it may be a monumental achievement just to get your feet firmly planted on the floor with your body upright. Even if that's all you've got, be proud of it.

Surround yourself with positive people. Counsel with fellow Christians. Get involved in a singles' group. Develop a network of friends, a variety of new people and interests.

Form friendships with other newly-divorced persons. Also, stay in fellowship with those who aren't divorced. Talk openly with people. Never feel guilty about asking for help, and don't allow anyone, not even your best friends, to make you feel guilty or beat you into the ground over what's happened.

Be active in your church. Be around loving people, those who aren't afraid to show their feelings and who can love without judging. Unknown and seldom understood by Christians is the need for nonjudgmental friends. This may even lead you to a change of churches—which some people are almost sure to misunderstand.

Keep looking to God! Life *will* eventually get better.

Be gentle with yourself! Recognize that the loss of a relationship does not diminish your personal self-worth or value. Try not to take a long ride on the guilt train. Learn to forgive yourself and others. Get lots of rest and exercise, eat right, *pray a lot,* and by all means try to maintain a sense of humor.

Take one day at a time. If that's too much to manage, take an hour, a minute, or a prayer at a time. But do whatever works! Say to yourself *twice* daily: "I did the best I could under the circumstances I was in and given what I had to work with!" (Say it now—and believe it.)

Lean heavily on God. "Faith in God has been my biggest salvation," said a young divorced woman, whose wisdom far exceeded her years. "Once I invited Christ into my life and began to focus on Him, things began to happen. I could see how He was working in my life."

Invite Jesus into *your* life. Ask Him to take control and to forgive your sins. "Therefore I say to you, all things for which you pray and ask, believe that you have received them, and they shall be granted you." Mark 11:24.

God saves us, not for what we are, but for what He can make of us. He sees what we can become. He longs to forgive our sins, to give us a clean start, and to fill our lives with meaning and purpose.

Chapter 2

The Demands of Living Alone

Pushed both by need and desire, I undertook the exhausting task of making a new life for myself and my children. Since divorce was my first major crisis as an adult, I couldn't form a clear picture of what my new life would be like or how I'd function in it.

Many months after my separation, I still asked myself, "Was separating the right thing to do?" I finally realized that the difficult decision had already been made, and the next logical step was to adjust my life accordingly. I now began to see how much energy, time, and effort it takes to build a new life following a severed marriage. Unfortunately, I could find no blueprints or set plans for this major endeavor.

I went through the motions of living. My body was there, but my mind was somewhere else. I spent every dinner hour in a daze. I couldn't eat, and I lost twelve pounds the first year. I looked like a skeleton. My eyes were ringed by dark circles. I lost all interest in my physical appearance. I didn't care whether I dressed, combed my hair, or put on makeup. I handled everything myself and refused help from anyone. I felt an enormous responsibility for my children, Tiffany and David. I knew I must be strong for them, and soon discovered it was absolutely necessary for me to stand up for them and myself, as no one else would. That isn't easy to do when one is falling apart inside. And I was.

My feelings plunged out of control, as if I were riding on an emotional roller coaster. Self-pity, doubt, and still more guilt surfaced. I viewed myself as a hopeless failure. Fears and frustrations coagulated inside, and I began to build a wall around myself.

I thought about the "special" wedding gifts my favorite aunt habitually gave to newlyweds: A tool kit for the astonished bride and a sewing kit for the equally astonished groom. Those attending probably shared my wonder. Shouldn't the gifts be given in reverse order? I now recognized the significance of her gifts. It was not her intent, of course, to prepare the newlyweds for a future divorce. On the contrary, she hoped they'd understand the importance of sharing household chores. My groom and I hadn't!

Now, as a lone female, I realized the difficulty each sex has trying to assume the responsibilities formerly carried by a mate. For me, financial burdens and car maintenance seemed especially insurmountable.

Although my husband and I had grown apart and our ability to communicate had already suffered a breakdown, his presence during our marriage camouflaged the fact that the entire weight of the household rested on my shoulders long before we separated. Now, that realization slowly eased my frustrations a little.

Overall, though, living alone proved to be very dismal. Unknowingly, I traded one set of problems for another. Demands, pressures, and even condemnation sprang up from totally unexpected sources.

I include the following experiences, not to complain or condemn, but because they may inspire an understanding for others in those who have never experienced divorce, and the knowledge that such feelings are normal in those who are now facing this crisis.

Neighbors

I stayed to myself. I could not relate to my neighbors or the happenings within the neighborhood, even though I'd lived in the same community for five years. I learned, much to my horror, that people I didn't even know had heard that my husband and I were separated. Those same people talked about me. The "neighborhood grapevine" is a powerfully destructive device. It seemed I was wrong no matter what I did!

I reminded myself every day that I wasn't responsible for the actions of others, only for my own reactions. I'm certainly not a martyr! Still I honestly believed my reactions should be in harmony with Ephesians 4:32: "Be kind to one another, tender-hearted, forgiving each other, just as God in Christ also has forgiven you."

Friends, Relatives, and Fellow Church Members

My friendships had been formed through the church and Christian organizations, so it was quite natural for me to look to fellow believers for emotional support and caring. Tragically, it wasn't there. The fact that I was only the second woman within our congregation to be divorced made it hard for people to understand my problem. To complicate matters, my former husband started dating the church's first divorced woman. Satan knows every weak spot! As a result of all this, I received very little warmth, acceptance, or compassion from my fellow parishioners. Even the pastor's efforts to help were apparently thwarted by members of the congregation.

Most of my Christian friends were very strict and rigid in their beliefs. They quickly told me what I could or couldn't do, without regard for my feelings. Some, being so "caught up" in the letter of the law, weren't able to love or accept me for myself, never mind separating the sin from the sinner. I bore the unbearable stigma of being a divorced Christian.

Emotional support—or the lack of it—from friends and relatives directly affects one's whole adjustment to the divorce crisis. Often, it's the children who suffer needlessly from condemnation. Children still need family, community, and church ties.

In retrospect, I can see that time supplies some healing factors in these relationships, but even time to heal passes slowly.

One lady I'd felt quite close to asked me to tell her all the details of our separation so she'd know better how to pray for me. Shocked, but trying not to respond in a bitter tone, I asked her just to mention my name as she prayed, and God would take care of the rest. And, of course, He *always* did!

I've always believed that true Christianity brings us to a higher level of righteousness. That most of my friends turned their backs on me when I needed them most reached far beyond the realm of my comprehension. Why did they do that?

Where Does One Turn When Christians Turn Away? The answer, I'm afraid, is at the same time simple and complex. One turns to God. I'm not suggesting that this is easy. It wasn't for me. Since I'm a flesh-and-blood person, I especially liked the comfort of other flesh-and-blood persons. Now, years later, I still don't understand why my Christian friends turned from me. It hurt! But God used negative circumstances in a positive way and drew me closer to Him. I learned to rely completely and unquestioningly on Him.

Business Dealings

Women, single, divorced, or widowed who live alone, must be especially cautious about hiring individuals or companies to make home or auto repairs. Being noticeably vulnerable, some people take advantage. Beware!

Somewhere along the way I developed the idea that widows were exempt from the worries of divorced women. But a widow friend told me that she, too, was concerned about the businesses she'd dealt with since her husband passed away.

"Women feel inept in several areas," she said. "They learn, from the advice of others or from their own sad experience, to be cautious."

Housing Discrimination

I felt compelled to move away from the house my former husband and I had shared. Since I didn't want to uproot the children from other familiar surroundings, I searched the newspaper ads for housing within our community. Most of the houses were too expensive. However, I found two prospective listings.

I dialed the telephone number in the first ad. A woman answered. I inquired and she told me all about the property.

She seemed very pleasant, and I was eager to meet her and excited about the possibility of having a new landlady. We scheduled a time to meet.

Before we hung up she asked, "How many do you have in your family?"

When I explained my situation, the whole tone of the conversation changed. The woman was polite, but her conclusions were obvious. She did not want a divorced person for a tenant.

Discouraged, I made the next call. The conversation was an echo of the first, except that landlord number two rudely declared that he didn't want "nothing like that in his home," and hung up on me. I was badly shaken. Why wouldn't they just see me or talk with me before assuming the worst?

Social Indigence

Society seems to condemn both the divorced and the poverty-stricken. Unfortunately, at that time I fit both categories. Poverty, plus needless condemnation, produced new anxiety within me. Thoughtless looks and comments consistently left me feeling degraded.

I suffered humiliation, weekly, as I shopped at the neighborhood market. Condemnation screamed at me whenever I used food stamps and Medicaid. One particular incident remains especially vivid. I was one of three customers standing in the check-out line. A young black woman was ahead of me. A middle-aged gentleman behind me watched intently as she paid for her groceries with food stamps. He continued to stare as she departed from the market.

"Everybody that uses food stamps drives a Cadillac," he said sarcastically.

The checker, who knew I also used food stamps, cast me a compassionate glance. Hours seemed to pass before my groceries were checked and bagged. I stopped breathing momentarily as I paid for my purchases with food stamps. I wondered, without looking back, what the man said after my departure. When will we learn how deeply our careless words and actions can hurt others?

Determined, nonetheless, I held my head higher, stood

taller, snuggled my children a little closer, and headed for my "Cadillac"—a twelve-year-old VW heap. I was thankful I'd parked right in front of the market.

As I looked into the faces of my children, I thanked God for His provision of food. And I reminded myself one more time that my children's care was my first concern. Regardless of public opinion, pride never kept me from fulfilling their needs.

Professional Attitudes

A genuine source of frustration came from dealing with professionals such as physicians and ministers who dealt with me purely on the basis of their perception of my emotional stability. I experienced several medical problems and went to my family doctor for treatment. He said that my illnesses were "all in my head" and that I had to expect these maladies because of my emotional state. He didn't even examine me!

On one such visit my arms and legs were swollen with giant hives. He insisted that the condition was a byproduct of my emotions and refused to treat it. After three weeks of intense suffering, I sought three additional medical opinions. One physician finally treated me from a physical, rather than an emotional viewpoint. Within two days the itching decreased, and the giant welts faded. In retrospect, I am not sure what caused the hives, but they were no doubt aggravated by my unsettled emotions. I was also suffering intensely, and for a professional person to refuse treatment merely because it was "all in my head" was, to me, the height of insensitivity. Admittedly, the physical treatment that was prescribed by another physician did not resolve the underlying emotional cause of the hives. However, it did relieve the symptoms that were causing me such intense pain, and at the moment of suffering, that is the bottom line, not the emotional cause of the problem which I, in fact, *did* undertake to deal with in time, as I was able to recognize the problem.

One of my neighbors suffered from severe emotional strain and asked me for help. I knew that I was not qualified to help her myself, and our congregation did not have a minister at the time, so I called another local pastor. During our phone conversation he at first agreed to visit my neighbor. However, out of courtesy he asked how I was getting along. I explained my situation, and suddenly he declined to visit my neighbor since he felt that my own emotional state had caused me to overreact to her problems.

His attitude infuriated me. I don't mean that Christians shouldn't turn to ministers when they are in distress because I've done this myself many times since, but why should my unstable situation at that time have kept him from inquiring about another human being's circumstances? During the next eighteen months my neighbor suffered three nervous breakdowns! Such professionals may have excellent medical and ministerial training, but they decide where they think these people *ought to be in their emotional and spiritual growth, and fail to relate to their patients or parishioners where they are.*

Legal Pressures

Three years passed from the time my husband and I separated until we petitioned for a divorce. He selected an attorney, an old family friend, who served us both. I learned the hard way that one attorney *cannot* adequately meet the needs of two opposing clients.

Much as I hated to admit it, I felt intimidated by my former husband. Also, the entire legal process terrified me. That, coupled with the fact I hadn't developed the ability to make my own decisions, caused me to make some very foolish choices. I tried to settle everything peaceably to preserve the relationship between my children and their father. While I didn't want alimony, I made the drastic mistake of settling for child support that was inadequate for one child, much less two. My children were cheated out of benefits they deserved by law. I learned later that I shouldn't have signed any documents that didn't provide reasonable child support.

I'm not suggesting that anyone "take" a former spouse for everything. The ex has living expenses too. But it's essential to provide realistic, reasonable child support and, if necessary, a temporary maintenance allowance for the custodial spouse until she (or he) can generate sufficient income.

THE DEMANDS OF LIVING ALONE

Our attorney advised me to petition the court to raise the support payments when the children were older and their needs greater. I did a few years later, but my petition was denied. However, the judge ordered my former husband to assume the children's medical expenses. That looked great on paper. Collecting was another matter.

Child support can be adjusted by either spouse through a court order any time a drastic financial change occurs, either by a windfall or by a dreaded financial disaster. That didn't apply in my case, though. While I was in financial distress, my former husband completed college and attended graduate school, and was usually a little worse off.

(See Appendix for Legal Tips.)

Suggestions for Meeting Daily Pressures

Develop a friendly relationship with God and seek His will. When hardships come, we often become bitter. But it's important that we accept the storm as well as the calm and continually submit to God's will. Seeking His will is a vital part of decision making, problem solving, and day-to-day living. Here are four of the ways I've found to do that.

1. Be open to His will. "Trust in the Lord with all your heart, and do not lean on your own understanding. In all your ways acknowledge Him, and He will make your paths straight." Proverbs 3:5, 6.

2. Study His Word. "Thy word is a lamp to my feet, and a light to my path." Psalm 119:105.

3. Pray. "Be anxious for nothing, but in everything by prayer and supplication with thanksgiving let your requests be made known to God." Philippians 4:6.

4. Commit yourself. "Commit your way to the Lord, trust also in Him." Psalm 37:5.

Learn to adjust to change. Promote a positive change. Things never stay the same. Adapting and adjusting to change is crucial to the life of a divorced person. Besides, making a change can be an exciting experience.

Don't be afraid to take risks. It's OK to be aggressive. Difficult times may require drastic measures for sanity and survival. If you make a mistake, view it as a learning experience instead of a failure.

Continue to develop skills that can be used in this fast-paced, rapidly changing society. Take the needed time, thought, and prayer to change your own life. The prayer by Saint Francis of Assisi has comforted countless generations: "God grant me the serenity to accept the things I cannot change, courage to change the things I can, and wisdom to know the difference." And I like to add, "God help me to do what's right even though it seems hopeless."

Develop decision-making skills. Pray for guidance. Allow God to be a part of your decision-making process. Knowing how to make wise decisions isn't something we humans are born with. It's a skill that's learned. As you master the skill, teach your children.

Gather pertinent information. Consider all the alternatives, goals, obstacles, and possible solutions. List all the advantages and disadvantages. Consult a friend or professional for *information*, but not for *advice*. Advice from friends may be good, but not necessarily tailored to your needs. Be a little skeptical of those who say, "If I were in your shoes. . . ."

Absorb the collected information. Make your decision based on the facts as you understand them. Sometimes a decision has to be altered or amended according to the need. Involve the children, as their age and level of comprehension allow. Remember, of course, that no decision will please everyone. Make your choice and abide with it.

Decide to be a survivor. The ability to survive or self-destruct is within each person. Realize there are certain things each divorced person must suffer or experience before the healing is complete. As you begin each new day, know without a doubt that you are one day closer to happier times!

Give hurts and injustices to God. When we give hurt feelings to God, they diminish in size. He will give the proper perspective. Don't allow bitterness, revenge, anger, or hatred to take over. These feelings are natural, and nearly always destructive.

Discouragement is the devil's best weapon! Don't give way

THE DEMANDS OF LIVING ALONE

to it. Continue looking to the Lord, for nothing is too hard for Him to handle.

All too often, we trudge along carrying hurts and injustices when we ought to commit them to the Almighty. See Psalm 37:5. When we commit something or someone to the Lord we give up our right to fret and worry about it. The following prayer from Ann Landers' column has helped me:

Merciful Father, I have been humiliated and hurt by a certain person. You know who I mean, God. You know, too, that I am struggling to keep bitterness and hate out of my heart, but it's so very difficult to find the grace to forgive. Will you help me, God? I don't want to crowd these bad feelings into the dark corners of my mind. I don't want to deny to myself the fact that I was hurt. But I do want to forgive and get the hostility and anger out of my system. At this very moment perhaps someone, somewhere, is having a hard time forgiving me for something I said or did. I might have hurt that person without even knowing it. So please, God, help me to forgive now. It would be terrible to harbor ill will against someone who might not even know he has hurt me.[2]

Forgive and forget. It's always easier to forgive than to forget. Romans 8:31 can help: "If God is for us, who is against us?" It's easy to focus on "who is against us," yet the focal point of the verse, "If God is for us," contains the deeper message. It doesn't matter who is against you when God is *for* you!

---

2. Ann Landers, Field Newspaper Syndicate, and the *Virginian-Pilot, Ledge-Star*. Used by permission.

Chapter 3
The Sting of Loneliness

At one time or another everyone experiences loneliness. This feeling intensifies with the death of a loved one or the breakup of a marital relationship, or any time intimate ties have been severed. For a divorced person, being without human attachment and feeling as if there is no one to rely on may seem closely akin to the "loneliness of the damned." Yet loneliness is not limited to the divorced or widowed. It hits the elderly, children, those in every economic level, in every part of the world, and, yes, it even strikes married people. Do you recall a time when you were married, but lonely?

I particularly recall one of many instances during my marriage when I felt overwhelmingly alone. My husband was a perennial college student who had time for everybody—but me. One evening I'd wanted to discuss the events of the day, but he insisted that quiet study was what he needed most. He studied until a sweet-sounding coed telephoned to discuss school business. Their trivial conversation (yes, it was trivial!) lasted two *solid* hours. No words exist to describe the pain I suffered that night.

Looking back, I can see that we divorced each other emotionally years before our physical separation.

In my mind's eye, I often pictured my husband as an island and myself a rowboat, but I was never quite able to approach the island or make contact. Emotionally, I was forbidden to get close to him.

Having experienced such loneliness during my marriage, I

didn't expect it to overpower me afterwards. My naive expectation was totally unrealistic. In fact, loneliness, even more than finances, became the worst part of my new life.

As I traveled through the emotional wasteland of a broken marriage, I withdrew from everyone except my parents and two close friends. I centered my life around my children. I actually believed that no one else cared.

As a result of my feeling of not belonging, I built a wall around myself. I no longer felt comfortable around couples, had little in common with single women, and didn't feel at ease with married women. Since I couldn't yet relate to other divorced women, where did I belong?

Fortunately, my two closest friends, Carol and Terry, offered their acceptance and support. I told them my innermost thoughts and knew that I could trust them. Carol, with her tremendous ability to see the humor in any situation, encouraged me not to take myself so seriously. Both friends were patient and helped me keep my sanity. When they couldn't pry me out of the house, they'd come over to talk or encourage me to work on crafts. Terry gave me an added interest by teaching me how to crochet. While these hobbies filled many hours, an emptiness still existed that couldn't be filled.

Weekends and holidays created another void. I found these "family days" almost impossible to get through. It was especially hard during the summer months when families gathered outdoors around their barbecue grills. Oh, how I missed that! I didn't have the energy or finances to do that myself.

I kept telling myself that others weren't having as much fun as they appeared to be. It was always a consolation, however slight, to remind myself that there were still many married women who were also lonely within their marriage as I once had been.

I occasionally ventured out to church functions and a Bible study, but it unnerved me to be in a crowd and still feel utterly alone. Since I carried a lump in my throat and was on the verge of tears much of the time, it was difficult to talk with other people. I found it particularly difficult to enjoy myself when people kept asking, "What happened?"

I *desperately* wanted to know what had happened myself. What went wrong? I spent many hours delving into the Scriptures and Christian books trying to discover what God had ordained marriage to be. I prayed and prayed, but sometimes I felt as if even God didn't listen.

Of course, my failure to feel God's nearness cast me into a deep depression. Reaching new depths of hopelessness and despair, I cried and cried—but couldn't explain my tears. Once, during a crying episode, I flung myself across the bed. How I got from the bed to the medicine cabinet remains a mystery. Yet I stood there with a bottle of pills in my hand. Looking into the mirror, I saw the face of a person I did not know. Startled, I asked, "What am I doing?"

I'd never before considered suicide as an option. I'd believed only a self-centered person would take his or her own life, though since that time I've known widows who felt the same way because of the loneliness, even though they were financially secure. I didn't want to be remembered that way. I didn't want my children to think I didn't love them enough to keep going. As it turned out, it was my children's love for *me* that kept me going.

I vividly remember another time when I was lying across the bed crying out to God, begging Him to let me know He was nearby. He answered immediately, sending David, then eighteen months old, toddling into my room to stroke my head. "I love ma-ma," he said in his baby gibberish. That warmed my heart and gave tangible proof of God's presence.

Although I spent my time caring for my two preschoolers, keeping busy and filling every minute of the day, coping with the nighttime hours was another matter. My loneliness escalated into sheer panic and terror. Fear *is* a lonely companion! Empty darkness filled long, sleepless nights and the expectation of danger came with every sound, no matter how slight.

Those sleepless nights, however miserable, afforded me the opportunity to reflect on our marriage. I remembered how difficult it was to lie in bed next to a man who didn't love me. That, I decided, had been much harder than sleeping alone.

Yet sleeping alone wasn't easy! Many nights I reached over

THE STING OF LONELINESS

to the vacant side of the bed, trying to comprehend that this wasn't a dream. It was real, and I was awake and alone. I'd loved married life. How I longed to again be held, hugged, and loved. I was starved for adult conversation, as well as for a man's point of view.

Sooner than expected, I was confronted with a masculine viewpoint, and I caught a glimpse of myself and my situation in an undesirable, negative way.

My church attendance had fallen to zero. Even the arrival of a new pastor failed to spark my interest. However, the new pastor decided to visit *all* the members of the congregation. His introduction was straight to the point. "Since you haven't come to church to meet me, I've come to meet you."

He invited me to church and encouraged me to get out of the house more and to consider finding a job. He was pleasant enough, but by that time, I just wanted to be left alone. Undaunted by my negative attitude, the pastor visited several more times.

Then his pleasant manner became brash and insulting. He compared my shutting myself up in my own house to being in a Hanoi prison. "Only this is much worse," he sharply rebuked, "because there aren't any locks on these doors that you can't open!"

He pressed his point even further. "The jail of your own making can be the worst—it's the one in your mind, the one you've constructed out of the anger you feel toward yourself."

I was stunned. I couldn't believe he'd talk to me like that.

Deep down I knew he was right, but I didn't know how to get out of this "prison of my own making." I hadn't learned how to stand on my own two feet. And I didn't need him to tell me that my adjustment to divorce was slow. I already knew that.

The new pastor embarrassed me to the point that I didn't want to see him again—but that didn't keep him away. He counseled me on how to find employment and how to turn my burdens over to God. (See the first item under Suggestions for Overcoming Loneliness.) He also advised me to seek more professional counseling. Since I opposed this idea, he agreed to help.

30 LIFE AFTER DIVORCE

As I look back on that time in my life, I believe God brought the new pastor and his family to our congregation specifically to help me. Figuratively, the marriage between "minister" and "congregation" didn't take. (Within eight months this pastor and his family transferred to another church.) But he definitely helped *this* member and her children! But during those few short months, his helping hand pulled me, sometimes against my will, out of the emotional rut that had consumed me. My whole outlook improved, and I saw things more clearly.

As the summer months approached, I decided, after much contemplation, to start looking for a job the following September. I could enjoy the summer with my children and begin job-hunting after Tiffany enrolled in school. I still didn't want to leave the children (Tiffany was now six and David, two and a half), but thought we'd try it for a while to see if it would work.

Soon, to my astonishment, I discovered that God had guided circumstances from the very beginning. I casually mentioned to a woman at the church my decision to search for a job. Several days later another member of our congregation, who was employed at a local hospital, called to tell me about a position that was open. She asked if I would be interested. I agreed to go for an interview.

Things happened fast after that. I had no baby-sitter and no wardrobe. It was only the first of August, and I had really wanted to wait one more month. I recognized, however, that it would be foolish to pass an acceptable job offer on that basis alone.

I called several people to locate a baby-sitter. A friend named Peggy said she'd like to watch the children. In God's gracious way, that immediate answer to prayer turned out to be better than I'd hoped for. I already knew that Peggy, a dedicated Christian, would provide excellent care for my children.

My interview went well, and I was terribly excited about the possibility of a new job. However, several days passed, and I didn't hear from the hospital. I called the personnel director to see if a decision had been made. It hadn't, but she told me that someone else had applied who had better qualifications and more experience.

My heart sank to my toes. However, before I had a chance to become more discouraged, the hospital personnel director called back to see if I would take the job. I hurriedly accepted and inquired about the other applicant. "She was overqualified and already employed elsewhere," the personnel director said. "We needed someone who could start immediately."

God, in His great wisdom, worked this out beautifully for me and the other applicant. Three weeks later, this other applicant was hired to fill another position in our office—one that perfectly suited her advanced skills.

As time went on, my children absorbed lots of love through their association with Peggy's close-knit family. Everything fell into place. With one phone call a new door had opened for me, and I'd moved into the working world. This seemingly inconsequential move was a giant step. I was confronted with a choice, prayed for guidance, made a decision, and followed through on it. God had listened.

A deeply imbedded sense of pride came to the surface. I felt good about myself. The world looked brighter, less isolated and lonely!

The Pleasures of Living Alone
The flip side of the loneliness coin is aloneness. There is a difference between loneliness and aloneness. It's possible to be alone and not be lonely. Periods of aloneness can be productive and creative. Comfort and peace can come from moments of solitude.

Many people choose the singleness as a permanent arrangement (see chapter 9) and cling to this appealing lifestyle, claiming God as their best Companion, but also claiming time for self-renewal, enjoying their own company, and being able to do as they please.

One friend of mine who doesn't even mind eating alone told me, "Solitude, itself, can be delectable."

The Comfort of Prayer
In the depths of loneliness and despair, when friends are not to be found, there *is* Someone waiting with outstretched arms

to give unending comfort. That Someone is the Almighty Father. First Thessalonians 5:17 attests that God is *always* listening and ready to hear our petitions. Paul says, "Pray without ceasing." While it's a good plan to have a specific time to pray, God is "on call" twenty-four hours a day!

Prayer provided the comfort I so desperately sought. God has answered *every* prayer. While I might not have understood at the time, every No answer was for my own good. As I look back, I'm thankful that God didn't grant some of my desperate requests.

I was surprised at how fast some of my prayers were answered. I learned never to be alarmed and never to give up, even if I didn't receive a quick response. I prayed five years about one request before receiving an answer. God *is* faithful; He did answer!

The Comfort of the Scriptures

Through prayer, I talked to God. Through Bible reading, God spoke to me. The Bible has been referred to as God's "love letter" to us. (See Appendix for "How to Use the Bible.")

Suggestions for Overcoming Loneliness

Make the Lord your constant Companion. Divorce, like any crisis, will be easier to get through with God on your side. "Draw near to God and He will draw near to you." James 4:8. Face each new day with the knowledge that He is nearby. In the midst of loneliness, it's vital to know that God will *never* leave or desert you. See Hebrews 13:5. Your most valued friends may let you down, but He won't. God loves you much more than any human can. Allow Him to be your Confidant and Friend.

With God's help, combat loneliness. Face it head on. There is no overnight cure. It takes hard work to fight loneliness and fill the void. Learn to have fun by yourself, to value the time spent alone. Be content with your own company—it's extremely healthy. Enjoy your new-found freedom.

Turn your burdens over to the Lord. You don't have to carry them alone. "Come to Me, all who are weary and heavy laden,

THE STING OF LONELINESS

and I will give you rest. Take My yoke upon you, and learn from Me, for I am gentle and humble in heart; and *you shall find rest for your souls. For My yoke is easy, and My load is light.*" Matthew 11:28-30, emphasis supplied.

Mend your broken heart. "The Lord is near to the brokenhearted, and saves those who are crushed in spirit." Psalm 34:18. Allow yourself time to cry. You can gain far more strength than you ever realized out of the most incredibly painful crisis. Learn to stand on your own two feet. Don't give up. *Don't give up hope.*

Accept the responsibility for making your life better. Develop a new hobby or pastime. In the evening, plan the events of the next day. This will give you something to look forward to. Become involved with church or community activities. If your church doesn't have a singles' program, start one.

Stop feeling sorry for yourself. Tell yourself you are OK! A broken relationship doesn't signal that something is wrong with you. Look at your good points. Thank God for creating you in His image.

There are several positive things you can do when depression moves in. Take a shower, dress up, and go for a walk or a drive. A change of scenery may help. Buy something, *within* your financial means, that will bring pleasure. There is no substitute for talking with a close friend, sharing a laugh. Get a physical check-up. Depression, after the breakup of a relationship, is normal. Being a little crazy is normal too. However, prolonged hopelessness and helplessness may indicate a physical ailment, as do sleep disorders, loss of appetite, and mood extremes.

Grief-stricken people the world over agree that the twenty-third psalm is extremely comforting. Read it often.

Make new friends. "We are all travelers in this world, and the best we find in our travels is an honest friend." R. L. Stevenson.

Reach out to others. Resolve to make new friends, those interested in understanding and loving you rather than using you. Cheer up someone who is lonely. Visit an elderly person. Do something for someone else. Be genuinely interested in another person. One understanding friend can be better than a psychiatrist or a tranquilizer.

Build friendships instead of walls. Allow yourself to trust again. Remember, it takes *time* to develop mutual understanding and trust. Be a friend without expecting anything in return.

Listen to others. Be available for a friend in need. Share your knowledge and skills. Be understanding—*not* critical! Praise and encourage a friend.

Manage the holidays. Do holidays make you despondent? If so, stop pretending that everything is the way it used to be or that everything is wonderful. Leave old, familiar traditions behind and begin new ones. If children are involved, allow them to help decide how the holidays will be celebrated.

Make definite plans for special days. Treat yourself to a nice, elaborate dinner. Visit friends or relatives, but don't spend the day alone or secluded.

Share yourself with others. Sometimes the best gift you can give your children is yourself. Wrap up a generous helping of time, energy, and caring. Tie it together with the ribbon of love and acceptance.

Get a good night's sleep. Abrupt changes in lifestyle may cause insomnia. Abnormal sleep patterns should be discussed with a physician if they persist. Here are some dos and don'ts.

Don't
- Use sleeping pills—they *are* habit forming!
- Discuss stressful family matters prior to bedtime
- Dwell on worries or troublesome thoughts
- Watch television programs which induce anxiety
- Drink caffeine-filled beverages

Do:
- Take a hot bath and relax
- Have a *light* bedtime snack
- Use a comfortable mattress and loose, comfortable sleepwear
- Keep the bedroom quiet and dark

- Use awake times to get something done. Perhaps you don't need as much sleep as you think
- Memorize Scriptures such as this one: "In peace I will both lie down and sleep, for Thou alone, O Lord, dost make me to dwell in safety." Psalm 4:8

Are you afraid? Call on the Lord to be your Shield and Protector. In His name, command Satan to leave you alone. Ask God to help you rest. When you put your head on your pillow tonight, *know* that you are in His hands! "You will not be afraid of the terror by night." Psalm 91:5.

Chapter 4
Are We Still a Family?

"You don't have a father anymore," I overheard a little boy tell my five-year-old daughter. I intervened, not only to explain to the boy, but also to reassure Tiffany that, indeed, she did still have a father.

While Tiffany seemed reassured, that young child's comment shot to the center of *my* broken heart and intensified my feeling that we were no longer a family. It amazed me that a comment by an innocent child could shake my sense of security. Sadly, in my fairy-tale-like dreams I still pictured the ideal family as husband, wife, and 2.3 children. Since God's procreation plan involved both husband and wife, I'd always believed that it took them both to raise and nurture a child.

I still believed it, even though I had questioned the validity of keeping our marriage together solely for the sake of the children. While the responsibility of raising children alone is great, the consequences are no worse than daily exposure to an unhappy marriage.

"Children can thrive in a happy environment, whether with one or two parents," my pediatrician confirmed. "A happy, single parent *can* give a child security."

As a single mother, my foremost concern was what lasting effects our broken marriage would have on our children. The children were also concerned about how a divorce would change their lives. Tiffany couldn't understand the difference between "foster children" and "natural children." She secretly feared, since Daddy and her foster sisters were gone, that I might someday give her and David away. I was stunned when she finally revealed what was bothering her. Getting the difference across to her was difficult, though, because I loved the foster girls as much as I loved my own children.

My daughter also thought her daddy no longer loved her. If he did, she rationalized, he would have stayed with us. "We *both* love you and your brother. You had nothing to do with our difficulties, and you weren't responsible for our breakup," I assured her again and again.

Having a "weekend father" was an adjustment for all of us. Tiffany and David became extremely excited when Daddy came to pick them up. They loved every minute with him. When the time to come home arrived, both children were tired and irritable. They cried and missed Daddy all over again.

I began to harbor resentment towards my ex-husband over these visitation times. He managed to "breeze in" for all the fun times and was "gone with the wind" on all the responsibility! We discussed this problem several times, but couldn't reach a workable solution. I'm not sure there is one.

Single parents often overcompensate. I tried to make up for the fact that my children didn't have a live-in father and that I couldn't provide special treats for them. As a result, I gave in to their every whim. Moreover, I found it difficult to be a strong disciplinarian and seldom made it clear what I expected from Tiffany and David. I was blind where they were concerned. They could wrap me around their tiny fingers—and they knew it! Many parents agree, in retrospect, that what was really needed was less indulgence and permissiveness. Now, I can see how wrong I was. Part of security is maintaining all the usual rules. *Children need and want a firm hand!*

Reflecting on my children's adjustment, I've recognized that despite being so wrapped up in my own grief, I guided them through various troublesome situations. And I know, without a doubt, that God guided me every step of the way.

The Fractured Family

Our promise to "love and cherish 'til death us do part" was broken and our family shattered. Guilty and unable to forgive myself, I realized that I'd married too young and for all the wrong reasons. I'd wanted, at age eighteen, to be on my own. Unfortunately, my generation of women didn't leave their parents' homes, get jobs, and apartments by themselves. I'm delighted that these options are available and acceptable for today's young women.

"Marry me tonight," my boyfriend said, "or you'll never see me again!" Too immature to understand that if our love was solid we could wait until we both had adequate jobs, I agreed. Two hours later, we became husband and wife.

Prior to our marriage, my former husband had suggested that if it didn't work out we could divorce later. That comment upset me, but I overlooked it, believing we could make it work. How deplorable it is that we make lifelong decisions without regard to consequences. But now the consequences had torn our worlds apart as we moved into the "absent father" and "overworked mother" status. How I missed having a partner. Our very first landlord lovingly referred to his wife as his "pot-na." I loved the sound of that word as it rolled off his lips. No one could say it quite the way he did. Now the memory of that word, and a love that once was, saddened me. This traumatic time produced many frustrations.

These frustrations spilled over into motherhood. I'd enjoyed every aspect of child-care, and I especially enjoyed feeding my babies while sitting in the rocking chair. One afternoon, while feeding five-month-old David, I sat stiff and rigid, tightly clinching my son and his bottle. When I finally looked down into his eyes, I saw a horrified look on his face. I immediately recognized my tenseness and loosened up. I started talking softly to him and stroking his tiny face, and he relaxed too. I didn't know that my son, at such an early age, could be tuned in to my emotions. From that moment on, I silently vowed to relax at feeding time.

Children and Divorce
My daughter Tiffany, then age seven, wrote a school report entitled "How a Child Feels About Divorce." Several sentences cut to the heart of my consciousness:

When there is divorce, your mother may see black in her head, and will not eat anything. Your mother will be so lonely. I know all of this because I have seen my mother been so uptight, and sad, but I didn't know what to do, but you might. If you love your mother, show it by helping her.

I wept uncontrollably as I read my daughter's perceptive homework assignment. It hadn't dawned on me that Tiffany had been so sensitive to my feelings. Since that time, though, I've discovered that parental ignorance of children's feelings is widespread. Yet children experience all the elements of normal grief, including shock, depression, denial, anger, low self-esteem, and shame.

In her *Virginian-Pilot* newspaper column, "Raising Children," Dr. Katharine Kersey, a professor at Old Dominion University in Virginia, stated the following:

Often children do not understand divorce. In the first place, many of them blame themselves and then, to make matters worse, they think they have it within their power to bring their parents together again.

Many couples use the child as a pawn. Some will not even talk directly to each other. They talk through the child. ("Tell your mother to buy you some new pajamas." "Tell your father I am tired of waiting for his check.")

As long as they are behaving like children, their children will model their immature behavior and will continue to be affected in many ways. They are likely to have trouble growing, developing, sleeping, eating, concentrating, behaving, and learning until their parents are able to get on with their lives—making peace with the past and dealing with the present and future in a productive and healthy way.[3]

---

3. Dr. Katharine C. Kersey, *The Virginian-Pilot* and *The Ledger-Star*. Used by Permission.

Who Gets Custody?

While 90 percent of all divorcing couples still agree that custody of the children should go to the mother, the sex of the custodial parent is less important. Times are changing. "What is in the best interest of the child?" is the determining factor, and often the child's desires are now being considered. Men are seeking and getting custody of their children. More and more women are freely giving up custody because they know their ex-husbands are caring, dependable fathers.

Nancy's Decision

Nancy was a close friend of mine who faced the decision of whether to leave her husband. "You are free to go," he said, "but I *won't* give up my son!" These words dominated the last few months of Nancy's failing marriage. Faced with the most difficult decision of her life, she sought religious counsel prior to leaving.

The counselor mapped out both sides of the issue for her, without being judgmental. "Once you decide," he advised, "you'll have to live with it, be firm, and stand by your choice. Divorce is fairly commonplace, but women who give up their children have extra pressures placed on them."

"I guess I knew from the very beginning that I couldn't take my son, Peter, away from his father," Nancy said. "I'd planned to move to another state, and I knew my husband would wither without him." She knew, too, that Peter, who had special medical problems, would suffer without his father. Nancy didn't want to disrupt his security by moving him away from his physicians or his school, which had special-education and speech-therapy classes.

Although Peter was nine years old, his level of understanding compared to that of a seven-year-old. "He listened well to my explanation, and his reactions were typical for a child whose parents were about to separate," Nancy said.

"What will happen to me?" Peter asked. "Will I have to move? Will Dad still be here? Will I get to see you?" Nancy assured him, but secretly she feared that she'd never see him again! She packed only her personal belongings, sat quietly

ARE WE STILL A FAMILY? 41

beside Peter's bed, kissed him, then left.

"Saying goodbye hurts," Nancy said. "Yet I knew my staying wouldn't have made it better. My son's development had stabilized, his routine had been regulated, and he'd passed the point where he would have to be institutionalized."

Nancy didn't know whether she could face other people after that. Her parents' reactions were typical. They allowed her to explain, but said in a state of shock, "We'll *never* forgive you for this!"

Other relatives were more helpful. Even when things appeared not to be working, Nancy's sister and grandmother supported her, never once suggesting that she reconsider her decision.

At first Nancy felt a new sense of freedom. Then, without warning, guilt erupted, and she felt like a failure. Friends, acquaintances, and business associates stoked that feeling whenever they asked, "What kind of a mother are you?"

"I've always wanted people to understand what it means to give up custody of a child," Nancy said. "It *can* work out favorably!" However, she admits that "you have to work hard to keep a positive attitude. Depression sits on your shoulder, much like the devil himself."

She had to learn how to defend herself, as well as to accept criticism without letting it bother her. "After all," Nancy says, "it's done; it's over; I can't fix it!"

Nancy visits her son three times a year, more often if necessary. "We share one-on-one quality time. I reassure Peter of my love and that I'm here for him," she said. "I also write lots of letters and call him frequently." Nancy recognizes that it's difficult to feel very much a part of her child's life when separated by hundreds of miles. "I don't get to do the things a mother gets to do. I've had to give up all my parental rights."

A real setback occurred for Nancy when her ex-husband remarried. She hated the thought that someone else was mothering her child. Nor did she realize that Peter's new stepmother was constantly making comments such as, "Your mother doesn't love you." Fortunately, Peter's father stepped in to rectify the situation.

Finally, after seven years, some very positive things have resulted from Nancy's extremely painful experience. "Peter's father is grateful for my decision to relinquish custody, and Peter has developed into a quality-functioning child. He works hard and is a self-sufficient sixteen-year-old.

"Almost everyone who truly cared for me, even though they may not have fully understood my decision, stood by me," Nancy says now. "Even my mother has witnessed how well Peter has turned out, and within the last year she has forgiven me." With a wry smile she also notes that one woman who at one time judged her severely has recently followed in her footsteps and relinquished custody of her child to her ex-husband.

"If I had to do it all again, I would," Nancy concluded. "Giving up Peter was the ultimate act of love. I believe I've made the right decision. Once the dust settled, our mother-son relationship improved. In fact, we now have a *great* relationship!"

Divorced Fathers Have Feelings (and Rights) Too!
Many noncustodial fathers are more than willing to actively participate in their children's lives, but some are forbidden to see their children unless their child-support payments are up-to-date. Others are never allowed to expand their fatherly roles and prove they can be just as capable, loving, and nurturing as mothers.

Many divorced fathers have little or no peer support. They struggle to manage with minimum parenting skills, and some even find it difficult to relate on an emotional level. Still, they try! But they face many roadblocks as they struggle to overcome these limitations. The biggest hurdle, most agree, is that they have to pay—without having any say!

Help for the Single Parent
University and community women's centers, as well as many hospitals and medical centers, offer special programs and seminars for single parents and women in transition. In addition, these institutions can often direct callers to a local

support group. One local college offers a noncredit course called, So You're Single Again! Many cities have crisis hotlines which provide twenty-four-hour emergency telephone service. Check your local telephone directory under the heading "Crisis Intervention Services." (See Appendix for helpful organizations and literature.)

Suggestions for Renewing a Sense of Family

Help the children heal their hurts. Allow your children time to air their hurt feelings and frustrations, to cry, or even to shout their disappointment. Make it absolutely clear to the child that he or she had nothing to do with the parents' breakup.

Prepare the children for their new lifestyle. Uprooting a child from familiar surroundings is threatening. He or she needs a stable, secure environment. The child's emotional well-being will more readily stabilize if *both* parents take an active part in their child's growth and development.

Don't take out your parental frustrations on your child. Never threaten to abandon your children. That's their greatest fear.

Help your children deal with problems at an early age. Unresolved problems don't go away. They hibernate and explode in the teen years.

Be on the lookout for radical or extreme changes in a child's personality such as withdrawal, poor school performance, insomnia, eating problems, or frequently claiming to be sick. Talk with the teachers, even if the child is doing well. Talking with a pastor, doctor, or professional counselor may help to pinpoint and prevent potential trouble.

Losing a parent is the most stressful thing that can happen to a child. You may have divorced your husband or your wife, but don't divorce your children. If you have an appointment to meet your children, be dependable. Whatever else happens, you show up! Assure the children about their futures.

Praise and *encourage your children.* They need to be valued. Thank them whenever they lend a helping hand. Tell them how well they've done. In all probability they have not done it as well as you could, but try to find some way in which they did well even if all you can say is, "I can tell you worked real hard on this and I'm proud of it."

Keep the channels of communication open. A good parent-child relationship is built on good communication. Talk freely with your children. *Listen* to them. Don't give up easily on dialogue. Try to get past one-word answers. Encourage a dialogue instead of a parental monologue. Give your full attention to the children. Be relaxed. Make eye contact. Lend a sympathetic ear. Find out their emotional needs and endeavor to meet them.

Be honest with your children, but don't let it be the kind of honesty that reveals all the sordid details. Don't be afraid to admit you've made a mistake, said something unkind, or wrongly fussed at your child. Don't be afraid to say, "I don't know," or "I'm sorry!"

Never say anything against the absent parent. Your children need *both* parents. Resentment, antagonism, and vindictiveness toward a former mate greatly disturb most children, even if they can't or don't express it. Ask God to close your lips against talk that will hurt others. Read Ephesians 4:29.

Continue to discipline. Stick with the discipline rules you used as a married person. Define limitations clearly. Children want to know where the limits are, even though they test them as hard as they can to see how far they can be stretched. Once the children's boundaries are defined, they can rest in the assurance that they are being securely supported by a strong parent. Sound easy? Don't count on it!

Succeed as a single parent. When your world falls apart, build another. Pray that you are the last divorced person in your family.

Provide your children with their basic needs: security, good food and shelter, love, forgiveness, self-worth, and esteem. Spend time alone with *each* child—at least fifteen minutes per day.

Include grandparents and other single-parent families in activities. Enjoy the good times and create new memories.

Don't overcompensate. It's natural for a parent to try to

make up for what is lacking in his children's lives, but, you can't *buy* what they need.

Don't force a child, either consciously or unconsciously, to take sides or to choose between his or her parents.

All parents make mistakes raising their children. Sometimes those mistakes are gigantic, but when children *know* they are loved, it matters less. Be confident. Be yourself! And, by all means, be the best parent God ordained you to be.

A word to the absent parent: Stay actively involved in your children's lives. They feel rejection from a missing or inaccessible parent.

Teach your children about God. "All your sons will be taught of the Lord; and the well-being of your sons will be great." Isaiah 54:13.

Introduce your children to God. Teach them to pray. Go to church *with* your children. Teach them that nothing can separate them from the love of God. See Romans 8:39.

Teach moral and Christian values. Be a good example. Remember that Christian values are learned at home.

Keep the channels of communication open to God. Pray for His guidance and for your children to be happy, loved, and free from fear.

Chapter 5

God's Constant Provisions

Financial stability is a great concern for most families, but for the single-parent family the search for financial security is monumental. How does a single parent achieve financial success when there is more "month than money" in his or her budget?

As one divorced parent said, "The financial burden is so severe that I have to worry, not about dollars, but about cents! I felt guilty spending a few pennies for soda pop. I just wasn't used to having money that was desperately needed elsewhere."

Most divorced women feel as if they live in close proximity to the "Poverty Zone." Men paying alimony and/or child support feel as if they do too. Second wives live in the same region.

Although I was working full time, it was a struggle to keep my head above the tidal wave of financial disaster. We still qualified for AFDC. The grant, however, was adjusted according to my monthly income. While I only received $25 a month, I retained the food stamps and Medicaid.

I had no delusions as to my ability to establish credit or to maintain the same standard of living I'd enjoyed in marriage. Nor was I overly concerned with luxuries. Yet, I continually strived to provide the necessities for myself and my children.

Strangely, in seeking financial independence, I learned that I had to become dependent upon God. I asked Him to show me how to manage the resources He'd provided. I also prayed for discipline and self-control.

In this "buy-now, pay later" society, it was too easy for me to yield to temptation. I was forced to learn how to distinguish between needs and desires. That was *hard*. It's so easy to justify a want as a need!

"Tell God your every need," said the leader of a Bible study group, "and He will fill the desires of your heart." She quoted Matthew 6:32: "Your heavenly Father knows that you need all these things." Afterward, she shared her personal prayer list with us. To my surprise and shock, she'd listed "wants" as well as basic "need" items.

"Well," I thought to myself, "that totally went against everything I'd been taught!" I truly believed I could ask God to fill our needs, but wasn't certain it was OK to ask for frivolous things.

In a skeptical manner I jotted down a few things I needed and some things I wanted. I told no one about the list. Still unsure, I prayed over my list once—feeling much like a small child asking for a new bicycle—and set it aside, somewhat afraid that lightning might strike (I didn't want to test or tempt God). Within one month, God provided everything on that list!

Watching the ways God moved, and the people He used, delighted me. He certainly filled all the desires of *my* heart. In fact, His provisions surpassed my greatest expectations!

God has provided for my every need. But, at this point, I must make a startling confession. I'm *not* a super-special person who deserves God's blessings more than anyone else. I'm a normal, hard-working woman who lives right here in Real World, USA.

Fortunately, God's Word and His promises aren't a fairy tale. They are real and solid, something that normal, everyday people can hold on to. I believe that. I've always believed that!

Yet, in the midst of one crisis after another, I've often felt like an orphan child that nobody loved. During those traumatic times, I've had to ask God to increase my measure of faith.

It's difficult (and that's an understatement) to be content or to think positive thoughts when the bills or other crisis situations seem bigger than life itself—with no way out.

I despise the words "Hang in there." I've hung in there, at times with only broken, jagged fingernails and a faith that was probably less than the size of a mustard seed (though I hoped God wasn't measuring!)

There have been times when everything was so bleak and I've been so panic-stricken that the only prayer I could utter, for weeks or months (depending on the situation), was "God, please help me!" During these times of distress, I've clung to one of my favorite Scripture verses. It's found in Psalm 37:25: "I have been young, and now I am old; yet I have not seen the righteous forsaken, or his descendants begging bread."

Financial Management

There are three steps that every newly-divorced person should take immediately in order to get his or her feet on the road to sound financial planning.

Step One. Close all joint accounts. Remove your personal valuables from a joint safe-deposit box. Establish new checking and savings accounts and insurance policies. If you are staying in the old house, have all utilities changed over to your name only. A deposit may be required.

Step Two. Meet with a financial planner. Set up a new budget. List assets and liabilities. How much money do you need? Can a current expense be cut from the budget? Is a part-time or full-time job necessary?

Step Three. Establish a savings plan. Budget an amount for savings, even if it's just a few dollars a week to start. The single mother, more than anyone else and regardless of the size of her income, needs assistance in planning for her and her children's future.

If you have minor children, it's advisable to have an attorney draw up a will. Designate who will take over custody of the children should you die, and establish a trust fund or insurance coverage for their care.

Check with the local Social Security Administration office for possible eligibility of benefits.

If at all possible, begin saving for your children's education. Open accounts for them. Perhaps your former spouse will "match" your monthly deposits in an education fund. Some parents set up this agreement in their divorce decree. One divorced woman told me quite emphatically that she sent her son through college by saving quarters and half-dollars. Her son also saved the money he earned working odd jobs after school. "You'd be surprised how fast that adds up," she said.

Child Support: "We Owe It to Our Kids!"

Child support is money contributed each month by the absent parent toward support of his/her children until they reach the age of eighteen. Unfortunately, in an effort to hurt the custodial spouse, many absent parents refuse to pay child support. Of course, it's the children who suffer, sometimes lacking sufficient food, clothing, or proper medical and dental care.

"If any one does not provide for his own, and especially for those of his household, he has denied the faith, and is worse than an unbeliever." 1 Timothy 5:8.

I struggled constantly to get my former husband to make his child-support payments. I received one or two payments after each court appearance. I'd always win in court, on paper, but saw very little in the form of checks or money afterward. (Fortunately, within the last two years, he has faithfully endeavored to pay his past-due child support.)

Sadly, though, child support is often *not* a source of income that the custodial parent can depend on. Court records indicate that a large percent of absent parents either refuse to pay or cannot meet the financial commitment.

How to Collect Child Support

Only 40 percent of all absent parents meet their child-support obligations. Of that 40 percent, only 10 percent pay on time and in full. Of course, these figures do not reflect the number of custodial parents who cease collection efforts. As one divorced mother said, "I just gave up! I felt as if I were fighting a 'no-win' battle for my children."

Nonpayment frequently brings about an economic disaster for custodial parents. It's difficult for them to plan a budget around erratic income. Most custodial parents don't have the resources and can't afford to lose time from work to track down the missing parent.

But don't give up. Keep trying to get what rightfully belongs to your children. Each state is required by federal law (Public Law 93-647) to set up units to help the custodial parent collect delinquent child support. It's essential that the custodial parent have the former spouse's social security number.

The Uniform Reciprocal Enforcement of Support Act provides cooperation between the states and helps custodial parents whose former mates have skipped town to avoid paying child support. Contact your local juvenile and domestic relations court.

One divorced woman recommends that the custodial parent "keep the channels of communication open between the child and the absent parent whenever possible. This may (or may not) ease the financial tension, but will provide a priceless contact for the child with a missing parent."

Some Fathers Pay, and Pay, and Pay!

Leshia, a friend of mine, renders an additional point of view:

"As a second wife, I was prepared to accept all the consequences of marrying a divorced man. I knew Tony had children to support, and that didn't bother me. In fact, we discussed and both accepted the child support commitment as our labor of love *for* Tony's children. However, we felt that his children were merely pawns in the hands of a vicious, shrewd, highly money-oriented woman. She is a professional whose annual salary had always been greater than Tony's—before the addition of child support. Every conversation and move she made was based on financial gain. She dragged us into court repeatedly to get more and more money.

"In court, she stood clad in designer clothes, shoes and purse, pleading poverty. She testified that we never gave Tony's children anything. The truth, to her, was that whatever we provided, including child support, was never enough!

"Paying child support has placed a tremendous hardship on our budget," Leshia continues, "but we've faithfully met our commitment, hoping that a sense of

GOD'S CONSTANT PROVISIONS 51

well-being will flourish in each child. Of course, we will continue with this goal in mind.

"Our hearts have been broken so many times, but what hurts most is that his children have been poisoned against us. We pray that as they mature, they'll see that life doesn't revolve around money and that our love will shine through all the untruths."

Tithing
Tithing is something I'd never given much thought to. I "knew" that God didn't intend for me to tithe on *my* meager income. I firmly believed He expected the more affluent church members to make that type of financial commitment. Not until I read Malachi 3:10 did I begin to suspect that God might be speaking directly to me. " 'Bring the whole tithe into the storehouse, so that there may be food in My house, and test Me now in this,' says the Lord of hosts, 'if I will not open for you the windows of heaven, and pour out for you a blessing until there is no more need.' "

This verse consumed my thoughts. I wanted to absorb its meaning to the fullest extent. My mind beheld a beautiful picture of God opening the windows of heaven and pouring forth prosperity beyond my greatest need. Notice the challenge to test Him. The Living Bible reads: "Try it! Let me prove it to you!" Most of my life I'd been taught *not* to test God. Nevertheless, there in black and white were instructions to do just that.

Indeed, God expected me to step out in faith and to trust Him. Since my decision to tithe, I've learned firsthand that if we give God His tenth, He will provide the other nine tenths. God has *never* failed to provide my family's every need.

There have been many times when a nonbeliever would have gone into shock after reviewing my budget, and there was one month when the budget cast *me* into a state of shock. In the midst of the monthly bills, I found one creditor that demanded immediate payment. It equaled the amount of my monthly tithe. My first thought was to let the tithe slide "just this once." In spite of my momentary lack of faith, I knew deep within my heart that only one choice existed. I paid the tithe.

52 LIFE AFTER DIVORCE

Three days later a refund check came from the power company for the exact amount of the bill! This check completely astounded me. I don't believe I've *ever* heard of anyone in our state receiving a refund (a credit on the bill perhaps, but *not* a refund!) from the power company. This served as another reminder of God's constant provision and how He is able to take care of every aspect of our lives.

Helping Others

Now, I knew that tithing was expected of me, and I could see that it worked. But, when confronted with the possibility that Christians should help others, I *knew* that God didn't mean me specifically. How could I help others when I lived from payday to payday? Then I read Proverbs 11:24, 25, LB: "It is possible to give away and become richer! It is also possible to hold on too tightly and lose everything. Yes, the liberal man shall be rich! By watering others, he waters himself."

In the final analysis, I firmly believe that the only way divorced mothers will be able to survive is by looking to the Lord and reaching out to each other with a helping hand. Together, they can share their surplus and conquer poverty.

Suggestions for Sound Economic Planning

Recognize God as the Origin of All Resources. Now, more than at any time in history, it's essential that we look to our heavenly Father for direction with money matters.

"God shall supply all your needs according to His riches in glory in Christ Jesus." Philippians 4:19. What He promises, He *can* deliver!

Don't be afraid to yield your resources and your life to God. Place your trust in Him, not riches! Ask for and accept His guidance. His wisdom is greater than ours.

"For the Scripture says, 'Whoever believes in Him will not be disappointed.' " Romans 10:11; emphasis supplied.

Practice Good Stewardship. Stewardship of the money that the Lord provides is the second step toward sound financial planning. "An overseer, then, must be . . . one who manages his own household well." 1 Timothy 3:2-4.

Tithing goes hand-in-hand with stewardship. Do not withhold from God that which belongs to Him already. Give with a loving and obedient heart. Tithing doesn't have anything to do with money, but rather with faith. It involves an unquestioning belief that God will take care of all our needs. We tithe because we love God and in order to acknowledge that He is the Source of all our blessings!

Share With Others. One way to open the window to greater financial fortune is to share the resources that God provides. Someone has said that "the real winners in life get what they want by helping others get what they need." Be sensitive to the needs of others. Be a cheerful giver. If you don't know anyone who is in need, ask God to show you someone who could benefit from your help or encouragement.

With whom does God expect us to share? "Give to him who asks of you, and do not turn away from him who wants to borrow from you." Matthew 5:42. "Let the man who has two tunics share with him who has none; and let him who has food do likewise." Luke 3:11.

Acknowledge God as the Source of All Your Abilities. God supplies special talents and skills according to individual need. "If any of you lacks wisdom, let him ask of God, who gives to all men generously and without reproach, and it will be given to him." James 1:5.

Ask God to reveal your strengths, talents, and abilities. Ask Him to give you wisdom in planning financial strategies or in whatever area your need exists.

Learn to Be Happy With the Provisions God Supplies. Don't dwell on the things you don't have, but concentrate on what you *do* have. "I have learned to be content in whatever circumstances I am." Philippians 4:11.

"Contentment is never the result of multiplying riches, increasing pleasures, or achieving fame. Even when they are obtained, one finds he still is not satisfied. Contentment does not depend upon things on the outside, but results from conditions on the inside! . . . To aspire to unrealistic goals or to grasp at riches that elude us will not bring happiness. Instead, with God's help we must do our best to accomplish our life's task with the talents and opportunities He gives us."[4]

Recognize One of God's Greatest Provisions. One of God's greatest provisions has no monetary value at all. It's the peace of mind that comes from the knowledge that we can rely on Him for everything and that everything comes from Him. Making money should never be the ultimate goal of life. The eternal investment that results from seeking first the kingdom of heaven reaps far greater dividends. Study Matthew 6:25-34. True wealth is the peace and inner security that come from God.

Accept the challenge in Malachi 3:10. Try it! Let God prove it to you! Watch the windows of heaven open and pour forth prosperity. Share with others and find contentment in the blessings God provides for you.

---

4. Henry G. Bosch, *Rainbows for God's Children in the Storm*, Baker Book House, 1984, p. 165.

Chapter 6

The Road to the Working World

Finances often dictate the need to work outside the home, either for the first time or by entering the work force after a long absence. Reentering the job market can be frightening for women who've been homemakers for a number of years. It was for me!

Like many working mothers, I had too much to do and too little time to do it. My working hours were from 7:30 a.m. to 4:00 p.m., but my morning began at 5:00 a.m. I had to get up early in order to get the children dressed, fed, and to the babysitter. While the early hours were very tiring, they allowed me more time in the afternoon with my children.

Work pressures began when our department head encouraged us to reach new effectiveness levels. She taught a medical terminology course and expected everyone in the office to attend. She also insisted that each of us reach our fullest potential by getting a job-related degree, which she said could be achieved while working full-time.

Though these programs were extremely valuable, they added more stress than I could handle. Time devoted to career advancement meant more time away from my children. I couldn't accept that consequence.

Added to this was the pressure to conform to a certain style of dress. The women in our office dressed to perfection. At times I felt too embarrassed about my attire to go to work—yet I had no choice. Although my appearance was important to me, I couldn't afford to keep up with every new fashion.

56 LIFE AFTER DIVORCE

Financial pressures extended right into the office. Employees were expected to contribute to every cause, be it a birthday, charity, or illness. While these were worthwhile, my budget was limited.

I tried not take my personal problems and frustrations to the office, yet at times I feared that I wouldn't learn to do my job efficiently or be able to keep up with the hectic pace. So, I repeated Philippians 4:13 over and over in my mind: "I can do all things through Him who strengthens me." God *is* sufficient. He got me through many days when I couldn't have made it alone.

The Balancing Act
"Once upon a time" . . . mothers didn't work!

The demands placed on today's woman extend far beyond traditional roles. She handles a great deal of responsibility, juggles two worlds, and needs super-human qualities.

It was especially hard for me to maintain a sense of balance. Success seemed beyond my reach. No one warned me how difficult it would be to deposit my precious cargo to the babysitter each morning and face another day in the working world.

Making it through each day depended on two factors: My relationship with God and my ability to stick to a schedule. A schedule was mandatory. Since my time off was promised to two little people, I only had a few hours a week to call my own, and I had to make the most of those hours.

Though I am a schedule-oriented person, I also recognized the importance of being flexible and open to God's direction for each day. Seeking God's guidance, through prayer and Bible reading, was essential. The more hectic my schedule, the greater the need to stay in touch with the Lord. On those days when my routine took the form of sheer craziness, I paused for ten to fifteen seconds at a time to ask for God's help.

Van, a friend of mine, was a newly-divorced woman with two children. I admired her apparent ability to blend pure faith with daily prayer requests. A contented, long-time homemaker prior to her divorce, she'd returned to her former profession in the accounting field. She told me that as she drove to work each morning she was keenly aware that she had to change roles. "It's tough to make the transition from my beloved role as a homemaker to that of a career woman in the blink of an eye," she said. Still, she seemed to be able to clear her mind of home and kids and direct her thoughts to highly technical data. At the end of each work day, no matter how stressful it had been, her thought process had to be reversed. "Most of my stamina is spent at work, and I don't have extra energy or patience," she said. "There isn't time to relax or unwind."

Van soon discovered, though, that it wasn't possible to maintain her earlier standards of housekeeping. She had to redefine her priorities. Now she prepares the evening meal and monitors the children's homework first, and sandwiches everything else in between.

"All the problems haven't been ironed out yet," Van told me the last time we talked about it. "Just surviving the morning routine took a great deal of planning, but I'm totally committed to making it work. Perseverance is vital!" Van says that when frustration builds to an intolerable level, she takes a "mental-health-day" off from work. "This allows me time to catch up with myself."

Van attributes her success to her faith in God. She says that in the midst of inward and outward struggles, and at times when she feels that she will falter, God literally brings her to her knees. "God is the sustaining power source in my life. I believe He will carry me through the days ahead and will help me fulfill my tasks."

Quality Time

Many single parents ask, "Do I spend enough time with my children?" I've often pondered that question myself. How many times have I heard that "it's the quality of time that counts, not the quantity"?

I've come to the conclusion that quality time is the time I spend with my children when I'm in tune with their emotional needs and am able to help them on that level. I know of no absolute rule about how much time should be spent with them, so long as it's on a daily basis.

Child Care

Adequate day care is the number one concern of the majority of working parents. Most confirm that work performance is better when they feel secure about the care their children are receiving. A qualified child-care specialist is someone who is *dependable,* caring, and responsive to a child's individual needs. The following points have helped me work out this important part of life.

What to look for when selecting day care. Check out two or three day care centers, nursery schools, or private sitters. If possible, visit each one for half a day. Ask for references, and verify the credentials. Don't be shy! Try to discover what it will be like for your child in each facility and the quality of the care he or she will receive. The cost, the convenience of location, and the staff-to-child ratio are very important considerations. Ask yourself these questions:

- Is the potential facility clean and adequately supervised? Are the toys clean? Is the atmosphere dismal or cheerful? Is there orderliness? Are shelves provided? Are there quality toys, bikes, and slides?
- Do the other children enrolled in the program seem content? What are they doing? Are they happy and active or glum and wandering around aimlessly?
- What activities will your children participate in? Are activities such as snack time and nap time scheduled?
- How does the baby-sitter/teacher respond to each child? Do the children receive encouragement? Is there discipline and organization?
- How are accidents handled? How are the needs of a crying child met? How is the temperamental, tantrum-throwing child managed?
- What provision is made for a sick child?

Security for Children of Working Parents

Children who are left at home while their parents work are highly vulnerable to crime. However, with proper planning, many of the crimes against children can be prevented. Accidents and home safety are also vital areas of concern. Teach your children what to do in the event of an emergency. Practice emergency procedures. Teach first-aid skills. Tell them what to do if their clothing catches on fire. (Don't run! Lie down and roll up in a blanket or small rug—anything that smothers fire.) Then, in the event of an actual emergency, the child will be better able to remain calm.

Caution your children not to open the door to strangers and not to tell telephone callers that they are alone. They should leave doors and windows locked.

Keep important phone numbers taped on or near the telephone. Include police and fire department numbers, your work number, the number of the noncustodial parent if he or she lives nearby, and a trusted neighbor or relative. Be sure the children know their own home telephone number and address. Teach them how to call home collect.

One child who stays at home alone (an older child) says, "No matter how independent or strong you are, you still suffer from loneliness. You feel like there's nobody at home that you can talk to or who can help *you* or who can fix things!"

How Children Feel About Working Mothers

"It doesn't really bother me that my mom works," said eleven-year-old Kristen. "I know *why* she's working."

Kristen's mother was divorced and has now remarried. Kristen stayed with a baby-sitter until she was eight years old. Now she and her brother, Kyle, fourteen, come home from school and are alone for one hour until their stepfather gets home from work.

"Kyle gets home first and then goes on his paper route," said Kristen. "Then I come home, put my books down, and call Mom. She asks how my day went and reminds me if this is the day I'm to clean my room."

Kristen is instructed to stay in the house and watch TV, snack, or do homework. "I was a little afraid when we started doing this three years ago," she said, "but I'm never afraid anymore. My mom works in a small office, so it's not like I have to go through ten people to get to her."

Both Kristen and Kyle have learned to handle phone calls, prepare a light lunch, keep doors locked, and *not* allow anyone inside.

"During the summer months, Mom lets my brother and me take turns visiting our friends," Kristen says. "We even get to go to the movies. I feel very secure with this arrangement."

By contrast, Rose, who came to the United States from the Philippines at age ten, also understood that her mother *had* to work. "I didn't like it, but there was nothing I could do about it," she said.

Rose baby-sat her three-year-old brother while her mother, a nurse, worked 3:00 to 11:00 p.m. "I was scared every minute and I missed my mom," she said. "I was sad and empty."

To complicate matters, Rose couldn't read or speak English. Her schoolwork suffered. Tired, confused, scared, and suffering from culture shock, Rose asked for extra help at school. She received three months of transitional help and finished the fifth grade during her first year here.

Nighttime was especially bad for Rose. "Every time I heard noises outside, I panicked and called neighbors to check around the house. They were always willing to help us.

"Mother left a list of emergency numbers by the phone, and I could always call her whenever I needed her.

"I've learned how to be on my own," Rose said years later at age nineteen, "but it was *hard!*"

Finding a Job

Preplan your job search. Make a personal assessment of all marketable skills. Homemakers, especially, tend to sell their abilities short. They should consider such attributes as financial planning, counseling, bargaining power, delegating, and refereeing. Remember that an organized homemaker will have an easier time stepping into the highly-structured work force.

Research the job market and consider each job's potential for advancement. Study the employment ads in the local newspapers. Visit your state's employment office. "Ask friends about job openings," advised a job counselor. "Often it's not what you know—it's who you know!"

THE ROAD TO THE WORKING WORLD 61

Follow all the leads. Prayerfully consider your options. Ask God to lead you to the job He has for you.

Write a résumé. The résumé is your introduction and is often your first contact with a prospective employer. Preparing it is an important part of the job search. Libraries and bookstores have volumes of material on how to prepare a résumé. Here are a few helpful hints:

- Include a cover letter. Find out the name of the personnel director or department head you will be working for at that company if they hire you, and address your letter to that specific person. In the cover letter tell which job you are applying for and ask for an interview. Thank the person for his or her consideration.
- List career goals, special skills, education, and employment history. Mention hobbies or activities that will enhance your future employment. It isn't necessary to include past salaries or reasons for leaving places of employment.
- Use action words such as *developed, negotiated,* and *supervised. Avoid negatives.*
- Include the names, addresses, and telephone numbers of all references. Ask each person you give as a reference in advance if it is all right to use his or her name. Be sure you have included your own name, address, and phone number!
- The finished résumé should be neat, clear, concise, and *free of typing errors or misspelled words.* The total length of your résumé should generally not exceed two pages. Make several copies and file extras for future use.

Prepare for the interview. The interview is your opportunity to sell your abilities and is the single most important part of searching for and securing employment. Act, look, and dress like a professional. *Do not bring personal problems to the interview!*

Arrive early. Go to the restroom and freshen up first. If you are asked to complete an application form, answer *every* question. Follow directions explicitly. Be accurate and neat. Answer truthfully. If a specific question doesn't apply to you, write N/A (not applicable) in the blank space.

Bring a pen so you don't have to ask to borrow one. Bring along the following information written down for quick reference: your social security and selective service numbers, all the schools you've attended (with dates), and a list of previous jobs.

Draw on God's power. Be confident, positive, attentive, and articulate. Be ready to tell why you want the particular job you are applying for and what skills and experience you can bring to it.

Succeeding at Your New Job

Assume the proper work attitude. Thank God for your job. Pray that He will give you the strength to meet your commitments.

Take pride in your work. Form responsible, dependable work habits. Be a conscientious steward of your time, talents, and energies. "Whatever you do, do your work heartily, as for the Lord rather than for men." Colossians 3:23.

Home crises can easily interfere with your work if you let them, but the following simple rules will help you to avoid this problem. *Don't* take personal problems to the office or confide in co-workers. *Do* talk with close friends, but not on company time. Choose a friend who will listen as you pour your heart out, and meet during your lunch time. If you feel like you're coming apart at the seams, seek refuge in the restroom. Practice deep breathing exercises. Maintaining a professional, businesslike attitude at the office will protect your job.

Create a work wardrobe. Plan your wardrobe carefully. Take stock of your current attire. Coordinate new purchases with existing clothing, such as buying one item that will fit with three others you already own. You can build a suitable wardrobe by purchasing one new outfit each season.

Determine what kind of working wardrobe will be most beneficial for you, then make a list of what you need. If you can afford it, seek advice from a fashion consultant.

THE ROAD TO THE WORKING WORLD 63

Develop your own image. Plan your wardrobe around your lifestyle. Discover which styles look best on you and are suitable for your job.

Keep your wardrobe purchases in tune with your budget. Insofar as possible, choose fabrics that can be worn year around and that can be machine washed. Buy a good pair of shoes and a purse. Use scarves, belts, and other accessories to update an older outfit.

Keep your clothing in good shape. Replace missing buttons and sew torn seams and loose hems. You can also use minor alterations to update an older garment.

Organize your life. Many chores can be assumed by children. Even the younger children can help with minor tasks. Clear your mind of professional duties on the way home from work. Leave the office and your co-workers behind. Whenever possible, plan some personal time right after you get home to pamper yourself: Take a shower, change clothes, and relax alone for a few minutes. During the remaining hours, enjoy your home and family members.

Don't allow your mind to wander back to the office to mentally complete unfinished work or resolve conflicts. Turn over any lingering problems to God.

When you're tired, everything seems worse than it actually is, so learn some relaxation methods. Get a good night's sleep and awake with a clear, refreshed outlook.

These suggestions may sound simple, but it's amazing how easy it is to overlook them in one's anxiety (panic?) to find and keep a new job. Following them should make your transition into the working world much smoother and happier.

Chapter 7
Feeling Good About Yourself

Low self-esteem seems to be a trait of many twentieth-century men and women. The trauma of divorce laid on top of such a universal emotion can strip away self-confidence. My own divorced life seemed to harvest failure. I couldn't find one seed of self-worth, and I couldn't grasp the idea that my life counted!

I'd been put down so much during my first marriage that I now had *no self-confidence whatsoever*. I had only shattered dreams and a shattered self-image.

The pastor's suggestion that I get additional counseling haunted me. As hard as I tried, I couldn't push his words out of my mind. "I'm *not* crazy," I told myself. Nevertheless, I was unable to control my emotions. Tears constantly erupted without warning. I finally admitted I was deeply troubled and filled with excessive fears, confusions, and unrelenting questioning.

After doing some research, I found that Medicaid would cover the cost of my therapy. Although I didn't have to worry about the expense, I was concerned about being away from my children one more hour each week. I wasn't just concerned; I hated being away from them. Though torn with indecision (old habits die hard!), I viewed Tiffany and David as a good reason to go. Since they only had one live-in parent, I reasoned, they certainly deserved one secure enough to take care of them.

Still, I wasn't sure!

As usual God was faithful to provide for my every need even

before I realized the need. This time His provision was a co-worker who'd previously been in therapy. She helped me to see that being in therapy wasn't anything to be ashamed of. "Psychotherapy is designed to help *normal* people with their adjustment problems," she assured me. Without her encouragement I wouldn't have kept my first appointment.

The first session lasted two hours—though it seemed like an eternity. The therapist, a licensed psychologist, asked question after question. We covered my entire life. I heard myself verbalizing things I hadn't thought about for years.

By the time the session was over, I felt as if my mind had been stretched beyond its limits. Afterward, it took several days to get myself together.

"It's important for you to set a goal and decide what you want to accomplish in therapy," the therapist had said. I didn't have a goal. I just wanted to prove to myself that I wasn't insane. It was hard for me to see that I'd been reasonably well-adjusted most of my life, becoming temporarily disturbed because of my crisis.

My psychologist was a man of great patience. During my two years of irregular therapy sessions (I couldn't see that they were doing any good), I fought him every inch of the way.

I was expected to do all the talking, to speak of anything that came to mind. Instead, I played silence games or figured out ways to draw the therapist into conversation. I was getting good at it, but he caught on quickly! I spent a lot of time stubbornly staring at the floor or the ceiling.

Eventually, I realized that his ability to help me depended entirely on what I shared. If I revealed half-truths, I could only expect half-effective treatment. That revelation did *not* come easily, but I gradually recognized that my therapist truly was on my side, and I was merely wasting his time and mine by constantly trying to outsmart him.

Once I learned to be totally honest with myself and my therapist and to hold nothing back, he helped me to focus on deeply suppressed emotions, the ones I'd been unable to face.

Analysis revealed that I was a very angry person. Instead of dealing with my anger, I'd held it inside because I thought "it was the Christian thing to do." I had to learn to communicate my feelings rather than holding them inside and to deal with my anger constructively—to release it without hurting others.

The most valuable lesson, if not the hardest, was to be totally honest with myself. It was *much* easier to suppress my true feelings and to fool myself into believing that no conflict existed. I'd developed an overwhelming ability to run from my problems. Of course, running from problems didn't solve them. In fact, wherever I ran, my problems followed.

Throughout my recovery period I kept a journal. I recorded my feelings, fears, problems, and possible solutions. I recorded both positive and negative thoughts.

Seeing my thoughts on paper gave me even greater insight into my own nature and into the problems at hand. By releasing pent-up emotions constructively I was able to deal with them more effectively.

A few years later, I had the opportunity to correspond briefly with my former therapist. Here is a portion of his letter:

> It was interesting to read your perceptions of the therapy encounter we experienced. I use the term *encounter* purposefully because I also felt the struggle. It is often difficult in my position to resist the urge to be directive and to "take over" the responsibility for the client's life and well-being, even knowing that is not best or therapeutic.

Years after my therapy encounter I understood how vital psychotherapy had been to my recovery. A friend of mine, Philip, shared with me what therapy had meant to him: "Psychotherapy gave me a foundation upon which to build a new life. I realized it was time to go back to being me."

I asked another friend, Bob, whether men suffer from a loss of self-esteem and confidence. "Yes, I'd say there's a real question mark about one's self-worth after a divorce," Bob said. "There's a little bit of that in *every* failure, because you wonder what you could have done to avoid it."

He went on to say that time, success in other things, and acceptance in other relationships had helped him. "I don't know if it was good luck, my job-related expertise, or whether it was because I buried myself in my work, but my job was going well and things came together for me professionally."

My friend C. J. expressed similar feelings: "The first few weeks after my wife dropped the bomb that she was leaving, I was in a state of shock. I wondered if I'd *ever* function again."

C. J. said that he especially felt the need for a friend to talk to, preferably a female he was not involved with. It needed to be someone he could talk to in order to rebuild his ego. "My special friend helped me understand what living one day at a time was all about," he said.

Several years ago I had an extremely exciting, albeit unnerving, experience. I was near an internationally known actress—a woman of great beauty, charm, and talent. During that brief time I accidentally overheard her relate some powerful feelings of insecurity to a mutual acquaintance. I was flabbergasted. How could someone of her fame and stature feel insecure?

I'd envied her in the past, thinking no one should be *that* beautiful. Now I empathized with her. I think God "allowed" me to hear what this woman said to show me that most human beings share feelings of insecurity regardless of how composed they may appear. I felt His love giving me more self-confidence from that day forward.

Rebuilding Self-Worth

Rebuilding self-worth is vital to total human fulfillment. It's an absolute *must* for the divorced person to deal with a lack of self-esteem and other emotional issues.

All of us are looking for self-worth. This seems to be the very basic need of our lives. It does not help for others to think we are worthy if we do not feel it ourselves. We need worth, but it must be *self-worth* if it is to be effective. What if God—the being of ultimate worth—came into my life and said, "You are worthy to me. I created you on purpose, and I am pleased with what I made. I love you." If that could happen and I could accept it, not just intellectually but also emotionally, I think it would make a profound difference. This is how God works. This is the power of the gospel. He came to make us feel loved and let that love make us feel worthy. The victory in Jesus is self-worth out of which everything else comes.[5]

Betty Jo is a woman of extraordinary courage. Her husband of twenty-two years walked out on her after she contracted breast cancer and had a mastectomy. She had to deal with both the terror of a life-threatening illness and a shattered marriage as well.

"Everything seemed to have been stacked against me," Betty Jo said. "Getting back into the working world after twenty-two years was scary. I didn't actually believe anyone would hire me or give me a chance."

Going into a potential place of employment and writing "none" in the work-experience section of the application blank took a lot of courage. Betty Jo is a beautiful blond with an outgoing personality, but she feared failure. She knew that she would have to take time off for chemotherapy treatments and five more operations.

Fortunately, someone *was* willing to give her a part-time job. "That was the first small step toward regaining my self-confidence," Betty Jo said. But she didn't sleep at all the night before her first day at work. "Self-doubt surfaced and tried to take my newly-found confidence away. Now that I had a job, I became concerned about *keeping* it."

However, as soon as she found out that she could do the work, her self-confidence returned and actually increased. "I'd lost my sense of identity somewhere along the way. It was a real comfort to discover that my brain wasn't dead and I could learn again," Betty Jo said much later.

The only way she's survived this multiple ordeal is through prayer. "I'm not one of those people who prays just at nighttime. As I drive to work I thank God for the beautiful day and offer many other prayers. I pray as well throughout the entire day. I repeat Philippians 4:13 daily: 'I can do all things through Him who strengthens me.' "

---

5. Adapted from Doug Manning, *With God on Your Side* (Hereford, Texas: In-Sight Books, Inc.), pp. 17-22.

FEELING GOOD ABOUT YOURSELF 69

Betty Jo concluded, "I'm working awfully hard, and I'm still going 'through it.' I don't know if you ever get over such tragedies. But prayer and getting my first job is what I needed to restore self-confidence. I know God is giving me the strength to carry on!"

Suggestions for Regaining Self-Confidence

Begin the journey to wholeness. "Look not mournfully into the Past. It comes not back again. Wisely improve the Present. It is thine. Go forth to meet the shadowy Future, without fear."—Henry Wadsworth Longfellow.

Pray for a miracle. Solicit God's help in getting your life on an even keel. Rise above feelings of personal failure. Accept your shortcomings. Pray for self-respect and confidence.

Seek professional help if you need it. Don't be ashamed to admit that you need help or that you don't have all the answers. It's your life. You *do* have the power to change it. You can't depend on anyone else for your own happiness. That has to come from within. God has the power to fill you with complete peace and happiness. He sent His only Son to save the lost and heal the brokenhearted.

Deal with anger. Anger is a God-given emotion to be used for survival. It is not evil. Express your honest feelings, but learn to vent angry feelings in a way that's nondestructive to others.

Anger turned inward leads to depression. *Don't bury anger—it will make you sick!* Deal with your angry feelings immediately. Don't deny that they exist and allow them to multiply into mountains of outrage.

King David expressed his hostility and anger in Psalm 109, keeping a "journal" of sorts. It's *not* an example of how to react when angry, but David vented his anger in writing, and that's good therapy.

This may be a good time to keep a private journal. It's OK to say things in your own private journal that you ought not to say to others. Be sure, though, that you keep your journal in a secure place. Family members and friends might not understand your darker feelings!

Ephesians 4:26, 27, LB, says, "If you are angry, don't sin by nursing your grudge. Don't let the sun go down with you still angry—get over it quickly; for when you are angry you give a mighty foothold to the devil."

Practice forgiveness, first with yourself, then with others. Remember, God loves us as we are, angry feelings and all.

Feel good about yourself! Learn to love yourself. Be around people who make you feel good. Seek the comfort of a loving, caring God. Try to take life's disappointments in stride. Find the positive in negative situations.

Concentrate on the things you do well. Sort out the talents and gifts God has given to you. Be proud of them and of yourself. God does not expect you to do things you are not equipped to do. Keep in mind that God made you a special, unique creature and that He loves you.

Learn to relax. Enjoy the time spent with your children. Derive satisfaction from simple, everyday pleasures. Stop to smell the flowers along the way. Daydream, think, walk on the beach, or play with your pet.

Help your children feel good about themselves. One of the most important tasks parents have is to help their children feel good about themselves. By loving our children unconditionally, we show them how God loves. Acceptance and praise help them develop self-worth. Without self-esteem they will not cope well with the disappointments of life.

Teach children how to overcome disappointments. Show them constructive channels for releasing their anger. When a child misbehaves, clearly state that you dislike his behavior, but that you love him.

A child must feel loved, nurtured, and valued. Say, "I love you," often. Show it in words and deeds. *Do you talk to your children the way you talk to your friends?* Shower them with attention. Show an interest in their friends.

Don't do everything for your children. Let them learn to take care of their own possessions. Foster a sense of responsibility. Allow them to make their own mistakes. Wisdom and knowledge can grow out of failure. Encourage them to keep trying.

Let your children grow up. That's the *tough* one!

Fill your soul with laughter. Laugh! Try not to take yourself too seriously. Laughter is an excellent release of anxiety and tension. It lightens our spirits, keeps us young, healthy, less nervous, and more fit.

Practice being spontaneous and jovial. Develop a playful spirit and free yourself from embarrassment. Instill a sense of humor in your children.

Be all that God created you to be. Believe in yourself and learn to accept yourself as God made you. "We are His workmanship, created in Christ Jesus for good works, which God prepared beforehand, that we should walk in them." Ephesians 2:10.

Recognize your own self-worth. Spend time getting to know yourself. Stay in touch with yourself. Stay in touch with God. Allow Jesus to shine through you!

Chapter 8

Sexuality and New Relationships

Friends, neighbors, relatives, church members, and even distant acquaintances encouraged me to date. I resisted all their "we-know-the-perfect-man-for-you" efforts because of my *definite* ideas about dating and remarrying. According to the way I interpreted Scripture, remarriage was out of the question. I knew if I dated, I'd meet someone and fall in love, and I just didn't trust myself.

On the other hand, I believed God truly created me to be a wife and mother. I loved my children and my home and desperately wanted to be a happily married woman.

My pastor advised me to review my feelings about dating and remarriage. He also compared me to the servant in Luke 19:12-26 who had buried his talents. "You are a very warm and caring person, and you should be proud of the talents and gifts God has given you," he said. "I know many people who would benefit from a friendship with you. There are many who need to feel that someone cares about them. For you to withhold love and caring is a greater wrong."

Oh, how I wanted to believe that he was right!

He further pointed out that I, more than anyone else, should realize that life is an endless series of risks. There were no guarantees that I would fall in love or marry again.

The pastor added, "I want you to see the importance of getting out of the house and involving yourself with friends and activities. View a date as a means of achieving this and nothing more."

I desperately wanted to follow his advice, but I still strug-

SEXUALITY AND NEW RELATIONSHIPS

gled with feelings of insecurity. Two years passed before I was actually back into circulation.

Friends introduced me to a divorced man. He was a tall, dark-haired, blue-eyed man who filled perfectly the "man of my dreams" image.

Our relationship, though, was more like a *bad* dream. At times I felt as if I were losing my mind. Something didn't quite add up. I felt confused and couldn't figure out what was wrong. Satan, the master of confusion, used my loneliness plus my naive, trusting nature to blind me to the truth—I was being used!

When our relationship ended and I discovered that the divorced man's looks were the extent of his desirable qualities, I was overwhelmed.

How could someone I'd thought a lot of reject me and I not see it coming? While the pain was as severe as that suffered after my divorce, it served as a catalyst. Emotions which had lain dormant since my separation released themselves and oceans of grief flooded out.

Then, as if dealing with new rejection were not enough, one of my neighbors cruelly stated to others that I was "one of *those* divorcées." Prior to my dating, however, rumors spread that "since I spent so much time with females, I must be lesbian!"

While both bits of gossip angered me greatly, I didn't know how to deal with them. For the first time in my life, I saw a part of the world I didn't know existed. I was shocked and disappointed to discover that not all people have sincere, innocent motives. On top of that, that there were men who lyingly said, "I love you," and never blinked twice.

It amazed me how eager some of my dates were to give up their "virginity" just for me. They wanted to play house but didn't want emotional ties or a ready-made family. Overcoming the "divorced woman" image that some men still believe to be true is difficult.

While my neighbors may have thought I was having the time of my life, I was busy trying to find new ways to fight off advances and to stay *out* of trouble!

Ninety percent of the men I went out with were undesirable.

74 LIFE AFTER DIVORCE

Yet with each new date, I secretly wondered if he was "Mister Right." Tiffany always asked if my date was going to be her new daddy. I had one date with a man who refused upon arrival to acknowledge that my children were even in the same room with him, much less take a minute to say Hello to them. I don't know why I even went out with him. The evening was ruined before it started.

Increasingly, dating became a strain. I had to be on guard every minute. I always wondered when and how the approach would be made. I couldn't enjoy myself when I constantly had to outmaneuver whatever planned strategy my date had in mind. Soon, I realized I was a poor judge of male character.

One man in my art class, who obviously considered divorcées to be unprincipled, invited me to go out with him after class. "Where would you like to go?" he asked.

"There's a pizza restaurant not far from here," I suggested.

"I know a place you'll like," he said.

Much to my dismay, he took me to a topless bar. I was humiliated. I'd never even been in an ordinary bar before, and I knew, without reservation, that I didn't *ever* want to go back to that one—or any other, for that matter.

The words, "Do not love the world, nor the things in the world" (1 John 2:15), kept running through my mind. "Surely, this bar must be what hell is like," I thought. "Why didn't I have the courage to say I wouldn't go into such a place?"

Sensing my obvious discomfort, my date apologized and took me home. I was convinced, after several bad experiences, that it wasn't safe to invite a date into my house after the evening's activities were over. Nevertheless, as I prepared to say goodnight to one date, he opened my front door and walked in ahead of me.

After one horrible experience, my baby-sitter and I devised a foolproof plan. I would tell my date I had to drive my babysitter home. It worked like a charm until one guy waited out on the street in his car for me to return. Imagine his surprise when my baby-sitter walked across the street to her home. Imagine my surprise when she called to tell me that he was parked a few houses away. I hurriedly switched off all the

SEXUALITY AND NEW RELATIONSHIPS

lights and went to bed. Needless to say, I didn't hear from him anymore!

My next date was a man I worked with. He was a pleasant person who genuinely seemed to like my children. He was polished, intelligent, and wealthy. He took me to the best places in town. He was quite a conversationalist. He seemed to enjoy talking to me as much as I enjoyed sharing my thoughts with him.

"There is no such thing as a free meal," my dad warned. "Everything has a price—even conversation!" He was right. There were always strings. It always boiled down to the same thing. And my explanation of wanting to save myself for marriage only provoked this wealthy conversationalist to anger.

He acted as if it was his "right" and "just reward" to have anything his heart desired, including me. Following my refusal came the verbal attack. His words ripped me to shreds.

"You are *worse* than a prostitute," he shouted, "because you are holding out for a wedding ring!"

Bitterness and a real disgust for men overcame me. "There isn't a decent man alive," I complained at work.

My co-workers laughingly teased me about getting so upset. "I would be insulted if my date *didn't* make a pass at me," one woman said.

How I longed to go out with one who *wouldn't*.

Eventually, I started dating a real gentleman. It was such a refreshing relief! I was relaxed and at ease, and my thoughts turned to love. We became engaged. For a while I was "on top of the world."

Gradually, though, little things impaired the fantasy, and the realization hit that I wasn't in love with my fiancé at all. I liked him, but I didn't love him. I wanted to. He was such a kind, decent man. I didn't want to hurt him, and several weeks passed before I gained the courage to break off with him—and he did feel hurt.

It also tore me apart at the seams. I was in love with love, or with the idea of marriage—but not with the man. When it was finally over, I decided I had had all I could take of any involvements. That was it. Finis!

Sex Without Marriage

As is typical of many divorced people, the sexual relationship in my marriage died several years before the marriage ended. It's natural for human beings, whether divorced or not, to want to know that they are attractive to the opposite sex and able to function sexually. I certainly wanted to know I was still desirable and lovable. That's what scared me! I was afraid I'd jump into bed with the first kind man who'd have me. I frequently reminded myself of Alexander Pope's words, "What reason weaves, by passion is undone."

I battled not only with my own desires, but with the added pressures placed on me by our current permissive society with its "whatever turns you on" attitude. Caught in the middle of a value crisis, I tried to sort out exactly what I believed about my sexuality in the light of my Christian convictions.

I read book after book after book, trying to learn how to deal with the issue of Christian sexuality and divorce. The issue was rarely discussed openly or honestly, even in church.

Human sexuality is a natural, God-given inclination. We are all created as sexual beings. The choice of how to use one's sexuality resides within each person. Nonetheless, all wisdom indicates that such a relationship should not be entered into lightly.

Consider the following statements from formerly married Christians, both men and women:

- I was lonely, relieved to be out of a miserable situation, and confident that God would give me the desires of my heart in His time. I knew this spiritually, but I had to let it become physical reality.
- I tried a love affair but found that celibacy worked when I prayed.
- I didn't deal well with my sexuality at all. I have many regrets. My actions didn't fit my moral standards. I was too intimate too soon.
- I'm not interested in a friendship without a sexual relationship.
- I had to learn that a relationship born out of passion cannot last—there's more to life than sex.

- I believe that premarital sex breeds mistrust in marriage. I have heard all the arguments *for* premarital relations. But sexual compatibility is something that couples work on "together" for years.
- You do what you have to do and hope that God forgives you.
- Giving in to sexual pressures and rationalizing to make sex OK under certain circumstances was harmful to my self-esteem. It also set up a pattern of interaction which destroyed relationships. Learning to love myself enough to trust God enough to provide my needs while saying No made me much happier, and consequently more popular. It enabled me to eventually build a healthy, wonderful second marriage relationship.

My own sexual character concerned me considerably. I mentally clarified my convictions, then asked God to give me the courage to live by them. His promise in 2 Thessalonians 3:3 encouraged me: "The Lord is faithful, and He will strengthen and protect you from the evil one."

Isaiah 54:5 has a very personal message for women. Read and meditate on it daily. "Your husband is your Maker, whose name is the Lord of hosts." God *can* fill your needs in special ways in the absence of a marriage partner. Believe it!

Suggestions for Building New Relationships

Meet someone new. Take control of your social life. Overcome shyness. Reach out to someone of the opposite sex. Don't be set back by rejection. Be yourself and develop your full potential.

Avoid isolation. You can't meet someone new if you're isolated. Singles meet in a variety of ways: through a mutual friend, while at work, through organized groups, or at small parties.

Don't simply focus on a person's outward appearance. Get to know him or her on an intellectual and emotional level. Look for likable qualities.

Get involved in an activity you enjoy. While you'll meet new people with similar interests, place the emphasis on *having fun* rather than *meeting new people*.

Seriously consider the ramifications of dating a non-Christian. "Do not be bound together with unbelievers; . . . what fellowship has light with darkness?" 2 Corinthians 6:14. You may think one date won't hurt anything—and it probably wouldn't if it ended there. But one date has a way of turning into two, and three, and on and on. Making a marriage work when two Christians are involved is hard enough! Pray extra carefully.

Help children accept parental dating. A child may struggle and feel abandoned and ignored when his or her parent begins to date other people. Reassure the child that his relationship with his parent is secure and that he does not need to feel threatened. Reassure him of your love for him.

And don't laugh at the child who attempts to be a matchmaker.

Children *must* eventually accept a parent's right to date. Assure the child that he or she will be the first to know if remarriage is being considered. Then keep that promise.

Express affection to others. Embrace freely, but with common sense. Verbally express affection in person, by telephone, or by sending a greeting card. Show mutual caring and respect. Sustain and affirm one another. Help a friend through a difficult time.

Ask God to show you ways to express affection.

Overcome temptation. As Christians, we all struggle at one time or another to overcome some stumbling block in our lives. Even though we may pray for victory, we still fail miserably. Forgive yourself if you fail. Keep trying and praying.

Go to a quiet place, seek God, pour out your heart's desires, and submit your will to Him. Then trust, Trust, TRUST!

"It is a trustworthy statement, deserving full acceptance, that Christ Jesus came into the world to save sinners, among whom I am foremost of all." 1 Timothy 1:15. We all sin daily, consciously and unconsciously, on purpose and without valid purpose.

Where there is sin, there is forgiveness through Christ. If you fall or even jump into sin, you don't have to stay there! "If

SEXUALITY AND NEW RELATIONSHIPS

we confess our sins, He is faithful and righteous to forgive us our sins and to cleanse us from all unrighteousness." 1 John 1:9. Fellowship with Christ will keep us from sin. Likewise, sin will keep us from fellowship. But it needn't stay that way for long. Accept God's forgiveness and forgive yourself.

Make a sincere effort to submit and resist. "Submit therefore to God. Resist the devil and he will flee from you." James 4:7. When faced with temptation, ask yourself:

1. Is it glorifying to God?
2. Is it good for me?
3. Is it good for those around me?

Stay close to God. Draw on His power. Persistently pray. Trust in God. Prayerfully consider:

1. 1 Peter 5:6-9
2. 1 Thessalonians 4:3-5
3. 1 Corinthians 10:13

I hope these suggestions will help you to establish rewarding Christian friendships as a single adult, and if God leads, to establish a new home that will be happier than the one you lost.

Chapter 9

To Remain Single or to Remarry?

Three years after my marriage ended, Sandy, one of my co-workers, asked me to meet a "real nice man."

"Oh boy," I thought, "here we go again!"

Sandy mentioned it several times before I finally agreed. A few days before the actual date, however, I broke out with a rash and was unable to keep it. I didn't know what had caused the rash, but my condition grew steadily worse. My ankles swelled to twice their normal size, and my legs and feet were blotched with giant hives. I could barely stand up.

The next three weeks of convalescing proved to be the turning point in my life—definitely my darkest hour. Perhaps God used this period of intense suffering and soul-searching to prepare me for the next stage in my life.

Several significant things happened during my illness. First, I examined my values and realized how completely they'd changed. Things that used to be important just weren't anymore.

My former husband and I had struggled to have the best of all material possessions. The more we got, the more we seemed to want. Yet all these monetary possessions hadn't brought us happiness.

"He who trusts in his riches will fall." Proverbs 11:28. We'd fallen all right, mainly because we failed to recognize that things weren't important—people were! We'd lost all concept of love, devotion, and respect. Deep within, where it hurts, I knew we had lived selfishly.

TO REMAIN SINGLE OR TO REMARRY?

The second significant event during my illness was to become painfully aware of the sin in my life. It seemed as if every sin I'd ever committed, since day one, came back to my mind. A sorrowful, sick feeling surfaced. I became impressed with the idea that no one develops so far spiritually toward God that he or she can indulge in even one sin without harm. Had my sins stemmed from selfishness, from wanting to fulfill my own desires above all else?

God's Timing

"There is an appointed time for everything. And there is a time for every event under heaven." Ecclesiastes 3:1.

Up to this point, "God's timing" had been a concept which held little meaning in my life. When I wanted something—I wanted it *right then.* I've learned since that God gives only the things that are good for us and when He knows that we are ready for them.

Patience was *not* my best virtue. Oh, how I wanted to marry again. I wanted that so urgently that I put my life "on hold" and believed it would be good again only after I remarried.

Since my illness lasted for several weeks, I had plenty of time to think and pray about a potential husband. Suddenly, I realized I'd been floundering from date to date, eliminating what I didn't want. But I didn't know what I *was* looking for in a future spouse.

I decided to make a list of all the physical, emotional, and spiritual qualities I admired. By the time the list was finished, I questioned whether such a "perfect" man existed. Convinced that he didn't, I subconsciously told the Lord I didn't want to meet anyone unless it was this perfect man!

Successfully Single

Gerri Young is one of today's women who chose to remain single after her five-and-a-half year marriage ended. She has successfully built a career and become a public affairs director in the U.S. Department of Defense. She is the very epitome of successful single womanhood. Beautiful and trim, Gerri, forty, is a remarkable woman. She owns her own home and expertly maintains the interior and the picturesque grounds. Here is Gerri's story, as she tells it.

> When I divorced in my late twenties, my mother was probably the closest person who watched me suffer through a tremendously painful time. All her encouragement started with the statement, "You'll find someone else." When friends offered encouragement, they frequently said, "There are other fish in the sea."
>
> A dozen years later, those two phrases are still offered by those same people. Though they mean to be encouraging, I seldom receive the comments that way.
>
> Underneath those two phrases is a subtle message. "You're a nice single person, but you'll be so much better as a married person," or, "You'll be OK if only you can find a husband."
>
> Society, starting with our family and friends, expects everyone to be married. The package is neater. Parties have even numbers that way. People today, even knowing our staggering divorce rate, still want to believe that marriage means security.
>
> During my twelve years as a divorced woman, I have been close to marriage twice. Once I had a diamond engagement ring on my finger for a brief and terrifying two days. The giver was a man I should not have dated, let alone married.
>
> In the early months of my present relationship, I found myself devotedly in love for the first time in my life. When I say I was close to marriage in this relationship, I speak only for myself. Marriage is not part of the gentleman's plan.
>
> With each long-term relationship termination, I suffer feelings of failure and rejection. I look around and see less remarkable females get married with ease, and I wonder what's wrong with me. I've been brainwashed to feel less than whole without a couple relationship. My family and friends add to my frustration each time they utter their well-meaning phrases.

TO REMAIN SINGLE OR TO REMARRY?

Maybe Noah started it all with his "two by two" business. His need to recreate God's creatures remains a basic need today. What is the one thing I simply must have if I wish to recreate myself? A mate. However, I currently don't wish to recreate myself. I'm past that point in life—never had a particularly strong desire to do so, anyway. What I want now is a partner who accepts me and encourages me and gives me room to grow.

Twelve years of singlehood have shown me that partners like that are rare. So should I spend my whole life pining away in search of the perfect mate to make me whole? What if I never find him? What could I have done for and with myself if I had channeled my energies elsewhere?

By channeling my energies into satisfaction with my life as it is, not as it might be, I can become, simply put, OK. I can accept that fairy-tales exist only on library shelves, that Sir Lancelot is not going to ride out of the sunset and sweep me away to that wonderful land of romance in the sky.

Instead, I can take care of myself, expand myself, and learn how to be happy with myself, feeling like a whole person who is fine alone but might be better with the right mate—not because of the right mate, but because of the kind of person I'd become before I established a new relationship.

I won't try to tell anyone that being single and alone is the best way to go. Nights and holidays can be lonely. Taking care of a house all by myself is exhausting. Having no one (a man) available when you need him can be depressing—but so can being married to the wrong man. (Sometimes even being married to the right man is depressing!)

Each condition of living has its pluses and minuses. What I'm trying to say is that it's OK to be unmarried. Having a husband does not make me a better person. I can make me a better person. The choices are mine.

Remarriage

During the two weeks that followed my illness, I'd planned to spend time getting back into the "work" groove. I was sure that my co-worker had forgotten about my agreement to date her friend. She hadn't! She arranged another time.

As the appointed time approached I got extremely nervous. When I looked through my picture window and saw Sandy's car in front of my house, my heart stopped up my throat and butterflies swirled in my stomach. I greeted Sandy awkwardly. She introduced her friend, Dick Foster, and his warm smile and kind appearance put me at ease immediately. Sandy, her husband, Harry, and Dick had planned our evening in great detail. We laughed a lot. Dick had a quick wit and an apparent zest for life.

By our third date I had discovered Dick to be a delightfully charming man. I tried to resist the feelings of love growing within my heart. So much bitterness still stemmed from my earlier unsatisfactory dating. My hopes of marrying had deteriorated, and I feared letting myself like him.

The first week of our courtship we talked and talked. We shared our thoughts, beliefs, hopes, and dreams. Dick was the only man I knew who ever spoke about "oneness" in marriage. That had *always* been my top priority, yet no one else seemed to understand or desire it.

Looking back now, I shudder to think how I resisted Sandy's efforts and how close I came to not meeting the man of my dreams. As usual, God provided in "His time," when He knew I was ready. I'd never thought I could love again, and I certainly didn't think myself capable of the love and respect I feel for Dick.

When Dick and I went for premarital counseling, our minister instructed us to face our new marriage with new hopes and new dreams and to put our past mistakes behind us.

Our courtship, wedding, and honeymoon were dreams come true. I think of Dick as my "made-to-order" husband. He's a composite of all the qualities I most admire. He's a man who dares to be different, to be himself. Kindness is his best attribute, but I must mention that he's tall, dark-haired, and has blue eyes that sparkle when he smiles.

I thank God that He didn't allow me take my life as I stood, long ago, in front of that medicine cabinet. I would have robbed myself of so much future happiness.

Happiness *did* come through my remarriage, but with the happiness came some *unexpected* adjustments. I secretly believed that the minute we were married, all the hurts and fears I'd carried in the past would disappear. It didn't work that way!

Second marriage couples face intense adjustments that don't exist in first marriages, and most couples tend to forget or overlook that reality. Sometimes couples have to work for years to straighten out personal problems and griefs brought into the marriage from the past. Added elements involve friendships, in-laws, step-children, discipline, finances, child support, and ex-spouses.

Sometimes, Remarriage is *Not* Made in Heaven

One friend, Martha, told me that she spent four years in withdrawal from society after her marriage ended. "I was angry, resentful, and fearful of a new relationship. I was afraid to make myself vulnerable to anyone. I regret that when I knocked down my built-in wall, I joined a church with no instruction in divorce recovery or relationship building.

"We were encouraged to pray, believing for answers. I prayed for contentment with being single, or for God to send a mate—according to His will. When a man I worked with started coming over, taking an interest in my son, attending church with me, and proposed marriage, I thought he was an answer to prayer.

"I married him without hesitation, thinking it was God's will. I still had no idea how relationships should be formed. Within a few months I learned that my new spouse had both alcohol and drug problems.

"Still believing our marriage to be an answer to prayer, I stayed with him until he left, four years later. Meanwhile, my son had discovered his stepfather's marijuana, and without my knowing it, had begun using drugs."

Suggestions for Finding Future Fulfillment

Enjoy life in the single lane. Your personal happiness doesn't depend on being married or unmarried. Don't put your life "on hold" until you find someone to marry. Stop thinking "poor me." Forget self-pity and wishful thinking. Don't rob yourself of the joy of being alone.

Live a positive life *now*. Don't think that all your problems will vanish if you remarry. They won't! They could even increase.

Fill the void in your life with God. Focus on the favorable aspects of your life. It's fine to realize that negatives exist, but get on with living. Focus on the beautiful creation God made you to be.

There *is* life after divorce! Enjoy yourself. Contentment is a state of mind. It comes from within a peace-filled heart and mind, not from circumstances or relationships, *except* for your relationship with God.

If you think of yourself as between marriages, read on: Consider the following nine rules which appeared in the article, "Don't Remarry in Haste—You'll Regret It" in the September 6, 1977, issue of *The Star*. The rules are still relevant today.

1. Avoid marrying just to ease the pain or loneliness of suddenly finding yourself single.

2. Learn to cope, on your own, with responsibilities that were formerly your spouse's. Many divorcees feel inadequate handling home repairs, money matters, cooking, and other chores, so they marry again to avoid them. This is not a good basis for a marriage.

3. Wait at least two and a half years to remarry. If you have a good relationship, the delay won't hurt. You're more likely to make a mistake marrying too soon than too late.

4. Take time between marriages to build your self-confidence so you don't bring too much emotional dependence to your new relationship. It can be deadly.

5. Be realistic about your intended partner. Divorced people tend to focus on qualities that their ex-mate lacked or to over-idealize the new person in their lives.

6. Learn to get through the bad periods of being single. Many people, though doing well as singles, suddenly hit one of those bleak periods where everything seems to go wrong at once. They marry impetuously for emotional support, then find themselves worse off than they were before.

7. Don't remarry if you expect to make changes in your partner. If you can't take him as you find him, leave him alone.

8. Discuss problems about your relationship before you marry. Don't expect them simply to disappear because you marry.

9. Be sure you choose a person whose personal values are similar to yours. Conflicting points of view about lifestyles and values ruin more marriages than any other factor. [6]

Whether you choose to remain single or to remarry, remember that both lifestyles have benefits as well as disadvantages. For now, the most healthy attitude is not to be obsessed with finding a new mate, nor setting one's mind against marriage.

---

6. Reprinted with permission from *The Star,* September 6, 1977, © 1977 World News Corporation.

Epilogue

Dick and I have been successfully involved for twelve years in what has been a second marriage for each of us. Prior to our wedding ceremony my friend, Vivian, advised me to enter this marriage with a positive attitude.

She suggested that I say daily, "We *are* married and we *can* deal with and work out anything that comes our way. Divorce will *never* again be a solution to any problem."

So, how are we doing? Have we achieved happiness and "lived happily ever after"?

NOT EXACTLY!

But, we *have* lived and loved our way through the necessary second marriage adjustments, my battle with breast cancer, my husband's job reversal and reduction of income, caring for my elderly father in our home, and so on. . . .

As my friend, Gerri, reminds me, "There are no more fairy-tales left in this life!"

Dick and I have a good marriage, but it didn't just happen—we've both had to work at it. In the midst of heavy trials (many of which neither of us had any control over) and numerous blessings, we have persevered.

With God's help, we've built a strong, solid union, one that is based, not on a fairy-tale, but on mutual respect, trust, commitment, hard work, love, and caring. And *that's what it's all about!*

Appendix

Agencies and Organizations

Check the yellow pages of your local telephone directory under "Social Service Organizations" and "Religious Organizations" for neighborhood chapters of the following organizations. Write or call individual organizations to receive further information. When requesting information by mail, enclose a self-addressed, stamped envelope.

America's Society of Separated and Divorced Men, Inc.
575 Keep St.
Elgin, IL 60120
(312) 695-2200

Association of Sleep Disorders Centers
604 Second St., SW
Rochester, MN 55902

Business and Professional Women's Foundation
2012 Massachusetts Ave., NW
Washington, D.C. 20036
(202) 293-1200

Child Care Action Campaign
99 Hudson St., Room 1233
New York, NY 10013
(212) 334-9595

COPE (Coping With the Overall Pregnancy/Parenting Experience)
530 Tremont St.
Boston, MA 02116
(617) 357-5588

Displaced Homemaker's Network
1411 K St. NW, Suite 930
Washington, D.C. 20005
(202) 628-6767

Family Service America
11700 West Lake Park Dr.
Park Place
Milwaukee, WI 53224
(414) 359-2111

Fathers for Equal Rights
P.O. Box 010847
Flagler Station
Miami, FL 33101
(305) 895-6351

Legal Aid Society
Civil Division
11 Park Place
New York, NY 10007
(212) 227-2755

Mothers Without Custody
P.O. Box 56762
Houston, TX 77027
(713) 840-1622

National Association of Christian Singles
1933 West Wisconsin Ave.
Milwaukee, WI 53233
(414) 344-7300

National Center for Missing and Exploited Children
1835 K Street, N.W., Suite 700
Washington, D.C. 20006
(202) 634-9821

A toll-free telephone line is open for those who have information that could lead to the location and recovery of a missing child: 1-800-THE-LOST

National Committee for Citizens in Education
10840 Little Patuxent Parkway, Suite 301
Columbia, MD 21044-3199
(301) 997-9300 Toll-free Hotline: 1-800-NET-WORK

National Committee for Prevention of Child Abuse
332 S. Michigan Ave., Suite 950
Chicago, IL 60604-4357
(312) 663-3520

Office of Child Support Enforcement
330 C Street, SW
Washington, D.C. 20201
(202) 245-1653

Office of the General Counsel
U.S. Office of Personnel Management
Washington, D.C. 20415
(202) 632-4518
If the former spouse is a federal employee (including military personnel), a social security recipient, or a federal retiree, this office will provide information concerning the designated agent to receive a garnishment order for child support and/or alimony.

Older Women's League
730 11th St., NW, Suite 300
Washington, D.C. 20001
(202) 783-6686

Organization for the Enforcement of Child Support, Inc.
119 Nicodemus Road
Reisterstown, MD 21136
(301) 833-2458

The YWCA sponsors a battered women's helpline and a group for battered women and their children. While this program is not uniform throughout the nation, the YWCA has 200 Battered Women's Shelters. If necessary, call your local YWCA for referral to the nearest shelter.

Books to Order
To obtain a copy of the *Child Care Handbook* send $3.95 plus $1.50 postage to:
Children's Defense Fund
122 C Street, NW, Suite 400
Washington, D.C. 20001
(202) 628-8787

Growing Through Divorce by Jim Smoke is an excellent book, but his "Guidelines for Successful Single Parenting" (page 60) are outstanding. This book can be purchased at a local Christian bookstore, or directly from Harvest House Publishers, 1075 Arrowsmith, Eugene, OR 97402, (503) 343-0123. Cost: $4.95 plus 75 cents postage, or ten percent of order. Credit card orders accepted: 1-800-547-8979.

Also available is a companion working guide to *Growing Through Divorce* by Jim Smoke and Lisa Guest ($3.95).

Free Booklets and Pamphlets
Consumer Information Center
Department 628M
Pueblo, CO 81009
Write for a copy of the "Handbook on Child Support Enforcement"

Federal Bureau of Investigation
J. Edgar Hoover Building
10th and Pennsylvania Avenues
Washington, D.C. 20535
ATT: Public Affairs Office
Offers a highly informative booklet "Crime Resistance"

Federal Trade Commission
Office of the Secretary
Correspondence Branch
Pennsylvania Ave., at Sixth St., NW
Washington, D.C. 20580
Offers booklet "Women and Credit Histories"

Helm, Incorporated
Publications Division
P.O. Box 07130
Detroit, MI 48207
Receive a list of "Sources for Automotive Materials" and a service publications order form.

Sex Crimes Unit, Detective Bureau
One Police Plaza, Room 1312
New York, NY 10038
The Detective Bureau's Sex Crime Unit of the New York City Police Department has put together two excellent pamphlets: "Children! Be Safe . . . Be Alert" and "Women! Beware . . . Be Aware." Write to request a free copy of each and include one letter-sized, self-addressed, stamped envelope for both pamphlets.

Shell Oil Company
P.O. Box 61609
Houston, TX 77208
Offers a series of booklets, "Do It Yourself Car Repair."

The U.S. Department of Labor
Women's Bureau
Publications Office, Room S3317
200 Constitution Ave., NW
Washington, D.C. 20210

Provides several publications about career choices for women.

How to Use the Bible
When in sorrow: Read John 14
When people fail you: Read Psalm 27
When you have sinned: Read Psalm 51
When you worry: Read Matthew 6:19-34
When you are in danger: Read Psalm 91
If you have the blues: Read Psalm 34
When God seems far away: Read Psalm 139
If you are discouraged: Read Isaiah 40
If your are lonely or fearful: Read Psalm 23
If you feel down and out: Read Romans 8:39
When you want courage for your task: Read Joshua 1
When the world seems bigger than God: Read Psalm 90
When leaving home for labor or travel: Read Psalms 121 and 107:23-31
When you want rest and peace: Read Matthew 11:25-30
If you get bitter or critical: Read 1 Corinthians 13
If thinking of investments and returns: Read Mark 10:17-31
For a great invitation—a great opportunity: Read Isaiah 55[7]

Legal Tips
Selecting an attorney is the single most important step a candidate for divorce will take. Unfortunately, major legal decisions and the selection of an attorney may have to be made when the client is highly confused and unsure of himself or herself. Ideally, the best time to consult an attorney is prior to the actual separation. Agreements will be drawn up that directly affect the rest of the divorced person's life and the lives of their children. Since the divorced person and his/her attorney will be working together at a difficult time, it's *important* to be selective.

Shop around for an attorney. Call your local Lawyer Referral Service (check state and city listings in the telephone direc-

---

7. Used by Permission. Newton Manufacturing Co., Newton, Iowa.

tory). Take the time to find an attorney who is compatible with your current needs. Check his/her credentials. No one is compelled to stick with an attorney who intimidates his client or who doesn't have the client's best interest at heart.

Hire an attorney (never a friend or family member who is in the legal profession) who is skilled in divorce cases and who is knowledgeable about current tax laws, or who is willing to be assisted by an accountant or tax attorney. Discuss the attorney's fee at the initial consultation and get an estimate of the total cost.

Never sign any legal document without first consulting an attorney. Know your rights and hire an attorney who, if necessary, will fight to preserve your rights. New legislation permits former mates to benefit from future pension plans. Spouses who put their former mates through college may be entitled to a percentage of all future earnings.